WOMEN IN LATE ANTIQUITY

Women
in Late Antiquity

Pagan and Christian Life-styles

GILLIAN CLARK

OXFORD
UNIVERSITY PRESS

This book has been printed digitally and produced in a standard specification in order to ensure its continuing availability

OXFORD
UNIVERSITY PRESS

Great Clarendon Street, Oxford OX2 6DP

Oxford University Press is a department of the University of Oxford.
It furthers the University's objective of excellence in research, scholarship,
and education by publishing worldwide in

Oxford New York

Auckland Cape Town Dar es Salaam Hong Kong Karachi
Kuala Lumpur Madrid Melbourne Mexico City Nairobi
New Delhi Shanghai Taipei Toronto
With offices in
Argentina Austria Brazil Chile Czech Republic France Greece
Guatemala Hungary Italy Japan South Korea Poland Portugal
Singapore Switzerland Thailand Turkey Ukraine Vietnam

Oxford is a registered trade mark of Oxford University Press
in the UK and in certain other countries

Published in the United States
by Oxford University Press Inc., New York

© Gillian Clark 1993

The moral rights of the author have been asserted

Database right Oxford University Press (maker)

Reprinted 2008

ISBN 978-0-19-872166-6

MIH et MTG
doctoribus doctissimis

PREFACE

IN the late 1980s I was teaching a course on women in antiquity for Classics students, and a course on patristic social thought for Theology students. The classicists (like some Greek and Roman writers) found it hard to believe that Christians were not a 'third race' but were Greeks and Romans too. The theologians were often shocked by early Christian teachings on women which were simply the cultural norm of Graeco-Roman antiquity. There was plenty for the classicists to read on women up to the second century AD, and for the theologians to read on women in the New Testament and apostolic periods. There was fascinating work coming out on beliefs about women, and about gender relationships, in patristic writings and late antiquity generally. But there was no general survey to take the Graeco-Roman story on and relate it to the patristic material, so I thought I would try to write one.

This seemed to be a modest and realizable project, but it soon became clear that much of the material was difficult to obtain or to interpret without specialist advice. My heartfelt thanks to the many friends and colleagues who responded to cries for help. I am indebted especially to Averil Cameron for her learned and perceptive comments on the final draft, and for help and encouragement over several years. The number of references to the works of Elizabeth A. Clark shows how much I owe, like everyone working in this field, to her writings. Antti Arjava, Jane Gardner, and Olivia Robinson improved the sections on law; Helen King, Vivian Nutton, and Noreen Fox improved the sections on medicine. Judith Evans-Grubbs, Jill Harries, Charlotte Roueché, Pat Starkey, and Roger White have made valuable comments, which probably seemed to them to be all in the day's work, but for which I am very grateful. Gill Cloke, Joanna Summers, and Ian Tompkins allowed me to read material, as yet unpublished, from their respective theses. None of these benefactors should be held responsible for errors unobserved or maintained.

Drafts of some sections were tried out at the Women in Antiquity seminar in Oxford, the Theological Studies seminar in Manchester, the Centre for the Study of Theology at Essex, and the Classical Association and the Women's Studies seminar in Liverpool. I am very grateful for all these opportunities, and particularly for the continued support and stimulus of the Liverpool group. The Sydney Jones Library of the University of Liverpool, and its excellent staff, supplied a remarkable number of the books and periodicals I needed to see; the Ashmolean and the Bodleian, the British Library, the John Rylands, the Hellenic and Roman Societies Library, and the Wellcome Institute for the History of Medicine provided the rest. Inevitably, books and papers kept coming out. I have not been able to make as much use as I would have liked of anything published after summer 1991, and I wish I could have used the books listed in the Bibliography as 'forthcoming'.

The most important acknowledgements come last. The book is dedicated to two outstanding teachers and writers of ancient history, Isobel Henderson and Miriam Griffin. Finally: without Stephen, Samuel, Dorothea, and Verity this book would no doubt have been finished in half the time, but life would have been much less interesting.

G. C.

University of Liverpool
1992

CONTENTS

LIST OF ILLUSTRATIONS

NOTE ON SOURCES AND TRANSLATIONS

Translations in the text and notes are my own, unless it is otherwise stated at the end of the quotation.

1. Patristic Texts

By convention, 'patristic' texts (otherwise known as the Church Fathers) are authoritative Christian writings, products of Graeco-Roman culture or strongly influenced by it, and dated after the apostolic period (first to second centuries) and before the medieval period (which may be deemed to begin at any point from the sixth to the tenth century). The most generally cited edition of these texts is that prepared and published by J.-P. Migne, *Patrologia Graeca* (PG) and *Patrologia Latina* (PL). Migne's editorial work is open to criticism, but the *Patrologia* is still the most widely available edition for those who want to look at the original text. In this book, patristic references are followed, wherever possible, by the volume and page number in Migne. Where no reference follows a citation, it should be assumed either that Migne has no usable text or that the text cited does not count as 'patristic'. In either case, the relevant edition will be found in the list of Short References.

Secondary works often refer to more recent series of patristic texts, especially *Corpus Scriptorum Ecclesiae Latinae* (CSEL), *Corpus Christianorum* (CC, or CCL for the Latin series), and *Sources Chrétiennes* (SC). Many, but by no means all, patristic texts are available in English translation: the major series are *Ante-Nicene Fathers* (ANF) and *Nicene and Post-Nicene Fathers* (NPNF); *Fathers of the Church* (Catholic University of America, abbreviated CUA); and *Ancient Christian Writers* (ACW).

2. Legal Material

There are two major collections of material, both made on the instructions of emperors. The Theodosian Code (*Codex Theodosianus*) is named after the emperor Theodosius I. The emperor Justinian is responsible for three collections of material: the Institutes, the Digest, and the Code (*Codex Justinianus*). The Institutes, Digest, and Justinian's Code are together known as the *Corpus Iuris Civilis*, a title assigned to them in the sixteenth century and sometimes used in secondary works with the abbreviation CIC.

Abbreviations vary. The Theodosian Code is abbreviated (as here) to CT, or to C. Th. Justinian's Institutes are abbreviated (as here) to J. *Inst.* or to I. Digest references are standardly D., followed by a string of numbers which indicate book, heading ('title'), section, and subsection; pr. means the preface of the relevant item. Justinian's Code is abbreviated (as here) to CJ or to C.

Several emperors added new legislation to their own or their predecessors' codes: these new items are called *Novellae* or in English translation Novels, and are abbreviated to *Nov.* with the name (in full or abbreviated) of the relevant emperor—e.g. *Nov. Anth.* for the *Novellae* of Anthemius. They are printed with the CT or the CJ depending on date. Some legal material also survives in the so-called 'barbarian codes' compiled by non-Roman kings for use by their formerly Roman subjects.

In this book, references to specific laws are followed by their date (given on the authority of the editions used). It is not possible to give an exact date for the comments by legal experts which are preserved in the *Institutes* and *Digest*.

Texts of the Theodosian Code and its *Novellae*, and of Justinian's *Institutes*, Digest, and Code with the relevant *Novellae*, are listed in Short References together with English translations. It should be said that the translation by S. P. Scott (1932) of the complete *Corpus Iuris Civilis* is not always reliable, so there is no satisfactory translation of Justinian's Code with his *Novellae*.

3. Medical Texts

Late-antique medicine was strongly influenced by two groups of texts which are not specifically cited in this book. First, the Hippocratic Corpus, which consists of Greek medical writings, mostly of the fifth and fourth centuries BC, ascribed to Hippocrates: references in secondary works may be followed up in the Loeb Classical Library edition (Greek text with facing English translation), *Hippocrates*, ed. W. H. S. Jones and E. T. Withington, 4 vols. (London: Heinemann, 1923–31), or, for some texts, in *Hippocratic Writings*, ed. G. E. R. Lloyd (Harmondsworth: Penguin, 1978). Secondly, the works of Galen (second century AD), who practised for a time in Rome but wrote in Greek. The text is usually cited from *Claudii Galeni opera omnia*, ed. C. G. Kühn, 20 vols. (Leipzig: Teubner, 1821–33); sometimes a text-reference is followed by K to indicate the use of this edition. Some works of Galen are available in English translation (details in Jackson 1988: 196).

The most influential writer on women's health was Soranus, a slightly earlier contemporary of Galen who also wrote in Greek: his works were translated into Latin (by Caelius Aurelianus among others) and circulated in abridged versions (by Mustio among others). His *Gynaecology* is available in annotated translation in English, and also in French with a facing Greek text (see Short References). Later medical writers include Oribasius in the fourth century, Caelius Aurelianus in the fifth, Aetius of Amida in the sixth, and Paul of Aegina in the seventh. English translations of some works by the last three, and a French translation of Oribasius, are also listed in Short References, but are less easy to obtain. There are editions of many Greek medical texts in the *Corpus Medicorum Graecorum*; these are individually edited volumes, and libraries often do not treat them as a series.

ABBREVIATIONS AND SHORT REFERENCES

Abbreviations

CCL	*Corpus Christianorum, series Latina*
CJ	*Codex Justinianus* (Justinian's Code)
CMG	*Corpus Medicorum Graecorum*
CT	*Codex Theodosianus* (Theodosian Code)
D.	Digest
ET	English translation
J. Inst.	Justinian, *Institutes*
JRS	*Journal of Roman Studies*
LCL	Loeb Classical Library
Nov.	*Novellae*
Nov. Anth.	*Novellae* of Anthemius
Nov. J.	*Novellae* of Justinian
Nov. Leo and Maj.	*Novellae* of Leo and Majorian
Nov. Marc.	*Novellae* of Marcian
Nov. Th.	*Novellae* of Theodosius
PG	*Patrologia Graeca*
PL	*Patrologia Latina*
PO	*Patrologia Orientalis*
SC	*Sources Chrétiennes*

Short References

(Excluding works in PG and PL, for which volume and page numbers are given in the text immediately after the reference.)

Acts of Paul and Thecla ET *New Testament Apocrypha*, ed. E. Hennecke and W. Schneemelcher, (London: SPCK, 1974), ii. 322–64.

Aetius

Aurelius Victor, *Caesars*

Ausonius, *Epicedion, Epitaphs, Parentalia*

Caelius Aurelianus

Caesarius of Arles, *Sermons*

Caesarius of Arles, *Rule, Life*

Claudian

Damascius, *Life of Isidore*

Dioscorides

Ephraim the Syrian, *Hymns*

Aetius Amidensis, *Iatricorum*, xvi, ed. S. Zervós (Leipzig: Teubner, 1901); ET (of Latin version) J. V. Ricci, *Aetios of Amida: The Gynaecology and Obstetrics of the Sixth Century AD* (Philadelphia: Blakiston, 1950)

Sexti Aurelii Victoris, *Liber de Caesaribus*, ed. F. Pichlmayr, rev. R. Gruendel (Leipzig: Teubner, 1961)

Ausonius, *Opuscula*, ed. S. Prete (Leipzig: Teubner, 1978)

Caelius Aurelianus: On Acute Diseases and On Chronic Diseases, ed. and tr. I. E. Drabkin (Chicago: University of Chicago Press, 1951)

Caesarii Arelatensis, *Sermones*, ed. G. Morin (CCL 103–4; Turnhout: Brepols, 1953)

S. Caesarii opera varia, ed. G. Morin (Maredsous, 1952)

Claudianus, *Carmina*, ed. J. B. Hall (Leipzig: Teubner, 1985)

Damascii vitae Isidori reliquiae, ed. C. Zintzen (Hildesheim: Olms 1967)

Dioscorides, *De materia medica*. ed. M. Wellmann, 3 vols. (Berlin: Weidmann, 1906–14); ET *Dioscorides: The Greek Herbal*, ed. R. T. Gunther (Oxford: Oxford University Press, 1934)

Éphrem de Nisibe, *Hymnes sur le Paradis*, ed. R. Lavenant

	(SC 137; Paris: Éditions du Cerf, 1968)
Eunapius, *Lives*	*Lives of the Sophists*, in *Philostratus and Eunapius*, ed. W. C. Wright (LCL; London: Heinemann, 1952)
Iamblichus, *On the Pythagorean Life*	*De vita Pythagorica*, ed. L. Deubner, rev. U. Klein (Stuttgart: Teubner, 1975); ET in G. Clark (1989)
John Chrysostom, *On Vainglory*	Jean Chrysostome, *Sur la vaine gloire et l'éducation des enfants*, ed. A. M. Malingrey (SC 188; Paris: Éditions du Cerf, 1972); ET in Laistner (1951)
John of Ephesus, *Lives of the Eastern Saints*	John of Ephesus, *Lives of the Eastern Saints*, ed. and tr. E. W. Brooks (PO 17–19; Paris: Firmin Didot, 1923–5)
Justinian, *Institutes, Digest, Code*	*Corpus Iuris Civilis*, ed. Th. Mommsen and Paul Krueger, 3 vols. (16th edn., Berlin: Weidmann, 1954); ET S. P. Scott, *The Civil Law*, 17 vols. (Cincinatti: Central Trust Co., 1932)
Justinian, *Digest*	*The Digest of Justinian*, Latin text ed. Th. Mommsen with the aid of P. Krueger, English translation ed. A. Watson, 4 vols. (Philadelphia: University of Pennsylvania Press, 1985)
Justinian, *Institutes*	P. Birks and G. McLeod, *Justinian's Institutes: Translated with an Introduction, with the Latin Text of Paul Krueger* (London: Duckworth, 1987)

Libanius, *Letters*	Libanius, *Opera*, ed. R. Foerster, vols. x, xi (Leipzig: Teubner, 1921-2)
Life of Melania	*Vie de Sainte Mélanie*, ed. D. Gorce (SC 90; Paris: Éditions du Cerf, 1962); ET in E. A. Clark (1984)
Life of Olympias	Jean Chrysostome, *Lettres à Olympias*, ed. A. Malingrey (SC 13bis; 2nd edn., Paris: Éditions du Cerf, 1968); ET in E. A. Clark (1979)
Macrobius, *On the Dream of Scipio*	Macrobii, *Commentarii*, ii, ed. J. Willis (Leipzig: Teubner, 1963)
Oribasius, *Medical Collections*	*Collectionum medicarum reliquiae*, in *Oribasius*, ed. J. Raeder (CMG 6. 1-2; Amsterdam: Hakkert, 1964)
Oribasius, *To Eunapius*	*Libri ad Eunapium*, (CMG 6.3; Amsterdam: Hakkert, 1964); French translation (with Greek text) in U. C. Bussemaker and C. Daremberg, *Œuvres d'Oribase*, 6 vols. (Paris: J. B. Baillère, 1851-76)
Palladius, *Lausiac History*	*The Lausiac History of Palladius*, ed. Dom C. Butler, 2 vols. (Cambridge: Cambridge University Press, 1896-1904)
Paul of Aegina, *Epitome*	Paulus Aegineta, *Epitomae medicae*, ed. J. L. Heilberg, 2 vols. (CMG 9; Leipzig: Teubner, 1921); ET Francis Adams, *The 7 Books of Paulus Aegineta* (London: The Sydenham Society, 1844-7)
Porphyry, *Life of Plotinus*	*Vita Plotini*, in *Plotini Opera*,

	i, ed. P. Henry (Oxford: Oxford Classical Texts, 1964)
Porphyry, *On Abstinence*	Porphyre, *De l'abstinence*, ed. J. Bouffartigue and M. Patillon (Paris: Les Belles-Lettres, 1977)
Porphyry, *To Marcella*	Porphyre, *Vie de Pythagore; Lettre à Marcella*, ed. E. des Places (Paris: Les Belles-Lettres 1982);ET, with facing text, in Wicker (1987)
Procopius, *Buildings, Secret History, Wars*	Procopius Caesariensis, *Opera omnia*, ed. J. Haury, 4 vols. (Leipzig: Teubner, 1905–6)
Protevangelium of James	ET *New Testament Apocrypha*, ed. E. Hennecke and W. Schneemelcher (SPCK 1974), i. 370–88
Sidonius	Sidonius Apollinaris, *Poems and Letters*, ed. and tr. W. C. Wright (LCL; London: Heinemann, 1936)
Soranus, *Gyn.*	Soranus, *Gynaecia*, ed. J. Ilberg (Leipzig: Teubner, 1927); ET Owsei Temkin, *Soranus, Gynecology* (Baltimore: Johns Hopkins, 1956); French translation of books 1 and 2, with facing Greek text, in Soranus d'Ephèse, *Les Maladies des femmes*, ed. A. Burguière and D. Gourevitch (Paris: Budé, 1988, 1990)
Stobaeus (John of Stobi)	*Ioannis Stobaei Anthologium*, ed. C. Wachsmuth and O. Hense (Berlin: Weidmann, 1974)
Theodoret, *Letters*	Théodoret de Cyr, *Corres-*

	pondance, ed. Y. Azéma (SC 40; 2nd edn., Paris: Éditions du Cerf, 1982)
Theodosian Code	*Theodosiani libri XVI*, ed. Th. Mommsen and Paul Meyer, 3 vols. (2nd edn., Berlin: Weidmann, 1954); ET *The Theodosian Code*, tr. C. Pharr (Princeton, NJ: Princeton University Press, 1952)
Zachariah, *Life of Severus*	Zachariah, *Life of Severus*, ed. and tr. M.-A. Kugener, PO 2 (Paris: Firmin Didot, 1907)

INTRODUCTION

The aim of this book is to give some basic information on women's lives in late antiquity, and to make a start on answering some basic questions: to what extent could women choose what to do? What social, practical, or legal constraints limited their choices? What options were available besides (or within) marriage and housekeeping? What was housekeeping like? What level of education or of health care was available? What conduct and ideals were women taught to admire?

Questions like these have been asked for the last twenty years, but most writing on women in antiquity focuses on the 'classical' periods of Athens in the fifth and fourth centuries BC and Rome in the late Republic and early empire; it is comparatively rare to find a book or paper which ranges beyond the start of the third century AD. There are good reasons why the second century AD tends to be a cut-off point, after which we enter what historians call 'late antiquity' and theologians 'the patristic period'. Political chaos and dearth of evidence make the third century, at least until the reign of Diocletian, a kind of lesser dark age from which we emerge into 'the Christian empire' with Constantine. Classical scholars suspect that Christianization brought profound social and intellectual change, even though recent work tends to emphasize the continuity of Christian with non-Christian teaching, the endurance of ancient traditions, and the unhelpfulness of calling people 'pagan'. New Testament scholars suspect that patristics is a different thought-world heavily influenced by Graeco-Roman philosophy, even though the express intention of the Church Fathers is to expound New Testament teaching. And, in purely practical terms, the source material is daunting. It includes the extensive collections of legal material assembled by Theodosius and Justinian; the Greek and Latin medical writers; and, especially, the voluminous writings of the Church Fathers. There is far less help available for interpreting them (or, for students with little or no Latin and Greek, simply finding out what they say) than there is for understanding legal or philosophical or rhetorical texts of the early empire—but there is a quite awe-inspiring tradition of scholarship on post-classical law, ancient medicine, and (especially) patristic theology.

Even so, the problems and possibilities of writing about women in late antiquity are not very different from those which apply in the 'classical' period. There is a wider range of cultural backgrounds which count as Roman, from Gaul to Syria and from the Danube to North Africa, and this makes it even clearer than usual that any synchronic, cross-cultural account of 'women's lives' is going to be misleading. It is, as usual, rare to have detailed information about any woman or group of women in any particular time and place, except sometimes among urban élites: Christian aristocrats in late-fourth-century Rome or mid-fifth-century Constantinople, for instance. What we do know about is 'discourses', the ways in which women's lives were perceived, interpreted, and (if possible) regulated in terms of leading ideas, priorities, assumptions, and interests.

The lawyers, doctors, theologians, creative writers, and artists who produced such discourses were (almost without exception) men, and were members of an educated élite with a common cultural inheritance. A few women shared this cultural heritage, but hardly any were heard (or expected to be heard) outside a circle of family and friends. Many historians respond to these problems by acknowledging that discourse—male discourse—is what they are talking about. But I think we need not be too pessimistic about the relationship of discourse to life. Discourses shape our perceptions, but also respond to what happens. Take the case of celibacy, which for much of the twentieth century has featured in a post-Freudian discourse of dangerous repressions. In the late 1980s celibacy was suddenly rehabilitated, in response to the spread of AIDS and the intense demands of some jobs. What people actually wanted to do, or were already doing, was validated by including celibacy in another discourse: that of taking control of one's life and time for what is most important to oneself. (Both this argument, and the argument that sexual activity can seriously damage your health, were very familiar in late antiquity: see Chapters 3 and 5.)

It does, of course, happen that discourses have a life of their own, and that assumptions continue unchallenged and unmodified by what is actually happening. This can be an occupational hazard of preaching (especially on Mothering Sunday). But many of the late-antique texts concerned with women are actually trying to deal with events: for instance, pastoral responses on difficult questions, or lawyers modifying the inherited rules in response to an obvious injustice or an unexpected problem. We can also, I think, often see why a particular response made sense both in terms of prevailing discourses and in terms of the facts. If a man's reason for marrying is not the wish to share his life with one particular woman (as in the discourse of romantic love) but the need to ensure legitimate heirs and a reliable manager of his household, and if an adulterous wife cannot reliably prevent conception by her lover, then the adultery of a married woman, or of a man with another man's wife, becomes a major threat to the security and transmission of property; so adultery is one of the most serious offences in late Roman law. By contrast, if the prevailing discourse is concerned with a child's duty to his or her parents, not with the child's right to life and development, and if it is also very difficult for doctors and midwives to distinguish deliberate abortion from miscarriage, the law may well keep quiet about abortion.

This optimistic view of what we can find out does not, of course, remove all the difficulties. Historians are quite rightly suspicious of 'collecting instances', especially when (as is usually the case) the instances belong in quite different contexts. Far less information survives overall about women than about men; and almost nothing survives of what women themselves wrote or made. Works written by women for public circulation are very rare, and there are none of the journals, letters, recipes, household hints, or designs for embroidery which have proved so valuable for later centuries. We are, as usual, trying to interrogate the writings and artefacts of men for information it never occurred to them to give. If we try to 'read against the grain', asking our own questions, there is no certainty that our dissatisfaction was shared by women of the time, whose experience and expectations were so different from our own. Even if it is accepted that we do have information about the past, all we can construct is a patchwork, piecing together scraps of material for a different purpose and to a different effect from that intended by their original makers.

The metaphor fails in that most fabrics in the ancient world were made by women; few examples have survived, and none complete. But one of the surviving works by a woman is indeed a patchwork. It is a *cento*—Latin for a patchwork cloak—by Faltonia Betitia Proba (PL 19. 803–18), which recycles Virgil as Christian scripture in hexameter verse. Proba did not challenge her inherited culture, except by being what she was: a woman with the technical literary skill to do this extraordinary thing, and with the Christian commitment which made it a reasonable use of her time and energies. She worked with the prestigious literary forms developed by men, and used them to make her different commitment acceptable and convincing. I find this a helpful image—and willingly admit that, when the methodology of writing history is so much debated, there is nothing like a good image to get the writing started.

This book is a patchwork in another sense. I have not read all the writings of the Church Fathers, or all the surviving legal and medical texts, or all the works of literature, or all the excavation reports, which might tell us something about women in the later empire; nor do I share A. H. M. Jones's confidence (1964: pp. vi–vii) that most of the relevant items in patristic writings are, in fact, well known. I have used material (to continue the patchwork image) from other work I was doing, and scraps from work other people have done, and I have looked around for more material to fill some of the gaps. This is not Log Cabin, or Boxes, or any of the other highly structured designs with interesting visual effects: it is the kind of patchwork in which pieces of a particular fabric appear in different places. Patchwork is a device for making something useful out of what you have, and if it looks good, that is a bonus. My sympathies are with frugal housewives, but I am quite sure there is more material to be found, and more patterns to be seen, by other scholars who are working with different interests and perspectives.

My own cut-off is the late sixth century. This is, perhaps, the beginning of the end of classical antiquity (cf. Averil Cameron 1991: 24), but my reason is simply that I do not know enough about the vernacular European cultures, or the Arab social patterns, which interacted with inherited Roman tradition. Fortunately, Late Antique and Byzantine studies are as spectacular a growth-area now as Women's Studies in the 1970s and 1980s, and other people are taking the story on into the later Byzantine and early medieval world and offering new comparisons and challenges.

I

LAW AND MORALITY

WHY begin with law as a way into women's lives? The law codes of any society tell us something about actions the society wishes to prevent and persons it wishes to protect. They do not tell us enough, because legislation has to deal in general rules which do not always match what people think or do. But late Roman law was presented in the form of the emperor speaking to his people. It is not written in the deliberately impersonal style of a present-day legal draughtsman, whose aim is to be clear and unambiguous—by those standards, it is quite startlingly emotional in tone and imprecise in content. The emperor responds to questions and protests, exhorts, scolds, threatens fearful penalties, or tries to explain why a change in the law is necessary.

Many of these changes occurred in family law, which had to respond to different local traditions within the empire, and also to social changes. The most important social change was the support offered by the Christian Church to women who did not marry, or who wished to give property to the Church or the poor rather than to their relatives; but the law also dealt with marriage, divorce, custody of children, prostitution and concubinage, adultery, and rape. The State is always concerned with the transmission of property and the stability of families and communities. To put it in the crudest economic terms, the State needs tax-paying households, and needs those in the higher tax brackets to stay prosperous. But economics is not everything: people, including emperors and their advisers, have strong views on the moral questions raised by ordinary family life. Should young people obey the decisions of their elders who foot the bills? Is it acceptable to divorce your spouse and remarry, to prevent or terminate pregnancy, to refuse to rear your child? How should property be left to avoid complaints of unfairness?

Since women in the later empire were, with very few exceptions, mostly concerned with private life, Roman law should give us some insight into what they did and what happened to them, what other people thought about it, and why there were changes in rules and practice. Surviving law codes and records of cases do reveal some of the changes over time and place which affected women's lives, but they have to be used with caution, for reasons which apply to research on women in any period of Graeco-Roman antiquity. First, our evidence for law and its workings is incomplete, and some geographical areas—particularly Egypt (Taubenschlag 1955)—are much better documented than others. Secondly, the evidence we have is mostly concerned with the more prosperous classes. Thirdly, almost all the voices we hear are those of men deciding what should be done by, or for, women.

Almost, but not quite all. Roman imperial legislation was sometimes prompted by the subjects of the empire. Women, like men, could ask the emperor or his officials for a formal legal response to a problem: many such 'rescripts' to women survive (Huchthausen 1974, 1976). But women were not involved as judges or legal experts in the making of law, and their appearances in court were restricted by social convention (Beaucamp 1990: 35–45). Constantine, shortly after he became ruler of the western empire, ruled that husbands might in some circumstances be agents for their wives, 'lest women, in their determination to pursue a lawsuit, should irreverently rush to bring the modesty of a matron into disrepute, and be forced to take part in assemblies of men and in trials' (CJ 2. 12. 21, AD 315). Women, evidently, continued to do just that. As ruler of the whole empire, Constantine reaffirmed what he held to be Roman tradition:

since the law is clear that women should not have the power to bring a public criminal charge except for specific causes, that is, if they are taking action on an injury done to themselves or to their family, the statutes should be respected in the old way. It is not right for women to have the power of making an accusation on every matter. But it has sometimes happened, in public trials, that their testimony, or their authority as accuser, has been accepted. Advocates should be warned that they must not, for profit, rashly accept as clients women who

may be relying on their sex and rushing into unlawful action. (CT 9.
1. 3, AD 322)

Incomplete, geographically patchy, class-biased, male-biased
evidence is nothing new for the Graeco-Roman world. But
law raises its own special questions. The existence of a law does
not prove either that people had generally been behaving in
the way it seeks to prevent, or that in future they will behave
as it requires. Legal status need not correspond to status within
society, and especially within the family. How much can the
content and procedures of late Roman legislation tell us about
late Roman society?

1.1. The Evidence

We have two major collections of late Roman law: the
Theodosian Code and the body of law—known since the
sixteenth century as the Corpus Iuris Civilis—assembled by
Justinian in the sixth century. The Theodosian Code is what
survives (incomplete, of course) from the attempt of Theodosius II, in the 420s, to rationalize the mass of inherited legislation and legal opinion which made the task of lawyers so
difficult. He decided first to assemble the relevant legal material and arrange it under headings, and then, when this task
was complete, to produce a second volume which would be a
clear guide for all his subjects on how they should live.
Unfortunately, the second volume never appeared.

In choosing material for the first volume, Theodosius and
his advisers ruled (CT 1. 4. 3, AD 426) that the last of the
great jurists—the legal experts whose opinions had primary
authority—were Ulpian (d. 223) and his pupil Modestinus.
This decision has had great influence: anything dated after
Ulpian still counts as 'post-classical' law, and, until recently,
has been exploited more for information about classical law
than as a source on late-antique society and ways of thinking.[1]

[1] For general accounts of post-classical law, see Jolowicz and Nicholas (1972:
ch. 27); Buckland (1975); Stein (1988); Harries (1988); Evans-Grubbs (1987, 1989);
Harries and Wood (forthcoming). Honoré (1978, 1981, 1982) discusses the work of
jurists and emperors: critiques in Averil Cameron (1979b) and Millar (1986). For
legal texts, see Note on Sources.

The Theodosian Code (published in 438) fulfils only part of Theodosius' plans. It is an assemblage of the imperial enactments ('constitutions'), from Constantine on, which were thought to apply throughout the empire. They are arranged under headings, so that we usually have extracts rather than the complete text of an imperial pronouncement; and they are accompanied by 'Interpretations', by persons unknown, which do not always make the purpose or the effect of the law any clearer. Added to the Theodosian Code are the Novels (*Novellae*), the new enactments of emperors from Theodosius to Anthemius (d. 472).

Justinian, who came to power in 527, thus had good reason to order a new codification of law. It was organized, by the jurist Tribonian, in three parts: the Institutes, a basic legal textbook; the Digest, a collection of authoritative opinions of the classical jurists; and the Code, which adds to the Theodosian Code some pre-Constantine legislation and some later material, much of it legislation by Justinian himself. Again there are Novels, legislation later than Justinian's Code; many of these are in Greek, the language of the eastern empire, whereas Justinian's Code is in Latin, as befits Roman legal tradition.

So what we have is an 'inherited conglomerate' rather than a consistent legal system, and this makes it difficult to detect changing social attitudes. The Theodosian Code does not survive complete. Where it does survive, it records (Turpin 1985) what Theodosius and his advisers found and preserved from the corpus of imperial legislation after 312; so for the state of the law before Constantine we almost always have to rely on reports in Justinian's collection of legal material. But both the Codes and the Digest rewrite, gloss, and omit in accordance with the needs of the time (Beaucamp 1990: 4–7, 341–7), and we do not have the original form of the material they reworked. We probably do not, for instance, have all of Constantine's moral legislation, and we certainly do not (Arjava 1988: 6–8) have a complete report of divorce law in the fourth and fifth centuries.

But the real problem is the relation of law to society. What prompted legal change, and did behaviour change when the law did? A new piece of legislation need not mean new social

patterns. Jurists may be interested in legal puzzles handed down
from past generations of jurists, rather than in what was actually showing up in the courts. Much of Justinian's legislation,
in particular, was prompted by contradictions and unclarity in
the material on which his law commission was working. On
the other hand, he (or the relevant adviser) does often explain
new legislation in terms of complaints which have been made
or abuses which have come to light. It is quite possible that
earlier legislation had regularly done the same, but that only
the specific provisions of the law were recorded in the
Theodosian and Justinianic collections of material.

But many family problems never came to court at all.
Surviving legislation sometimes acknowledges its own irrelevance to the poor, who, in the eastern empire, would have
had to hire a lawyer just to make sense of a Latin law code. The
leading law schools at Berytus (until the earthquake of 551)
and Constantinople (from 535) based their teaching on Latin
texts, but not even their students could cope: teachers had to
issue paraphrases and translations of the Digest (Scheltema
1967), and eastern emperors from Leo on recognized the need to
legislate in Greek (see Honoré (1978: 39) for the proportions
of Greek and Latin in texts and teaching). Even without the
language problem, there was a financial barrier. The more
prosperous classes, who made written contracts of marriage
long before it was required in law (Wolff 1950: 291–3), were
much more likely to be up to date on what the law was, or to
request an official opinion—not that the opinion would necessarily be correct, if the official they asked was ignorant or
corrupt. Or the official might have due regard for a local
tradition which did not correspond to the latest imperial
pronouncement. Any of these reasons may explain why in
Egypt, where documentation is as always much richer than in
other parts of the empire, we still cannot match the surviving
records to changes in the law on divorce between the fourth
and sixth centuries (Bagnall 1987: 54–7).[2]

When people did ask a question of the emperor, or a case did
come to court, one person's problem could bring about legal

---

[2] Beaucamp (1990. 4–5) notes the gap between imperial legislation and the
papyri, on which she promises a second volume.

change. A written decision ('rescript') of the emperor had the force of law. From the late third century on, greater efforts were made to ensure that imperial responses on particular cases were generally applicable, and they were presented in the form of a general law (Harries 1988). Thus a law might be prompted by a cause célèbre, or a sudden shocked discovery, rather than by awareness of widespread social change. It may also reflect an emperor's immediate reaction rather than a jurist's considered response; but jurists are human too, and one man's lobbying may achieve a law, just as one man's style may determine its drafting even when it has been through committee stages. When we use the shorthand 'Constantine decreed' or 'Justinian declared', we may be almost correct, and there are detectable differences between the two reigns. But, on the other hand, we cannot assume that the relevant emperor was personally committed to a programme of legislation, or even (in times when there was more than one emperor) that he had seen the law to which his name was attached.

To take a dramatic example: a law of Constantine (CT 9. 24. 1, AD 320) denounces, with lavish rhetoric, those who connive at an abduction marriage—that is, the snatching of a woman (who may well have been part of the plot) so that her family has to agree to the marriage. This is no proof that abduction marriages were on the increase early in the fourth century (Evans-Grubbs 1989: 81–2), or that the outraged tone and savage penalties of the law reveal a general feeling. It may have been the personal conviction of the emperor Constantine that families should not be forced into consent, especially when the bride had not been a helpless victim but had conspired to out-manœuvre them. But it may also be the case that Constantine spoke for a body of provincial public opinion which had not previously influenced Roman law.

But opinion differed over time and place. When Basil, bishop of Caesarea (*Letter* 199. 22, PG 32. 721), was asked for an opinion on abduction marriage, half a century later, abductions were still happening, and Basil's reaction is quite different from Constantine's law: the woman must be returned to her fiancé if she has one, otherwise to her family, and they must decide whether to keep her or concede her to the abductor. It appears that, if the family accepted marriage to the abductor, so would the Church. There was no standard penance for abduction (see below, Sect. 2.3), and, if there had been neither seduction nor violence, there was no serious problem (cf. Basil, *Letter* 199. 30 on the case of a widow). Where Constantine is angered on behalf of the father who has the legal right to assign his daughter and his property, Basil is looking for a peaceful solution.

But Basil's response cannot be generalized as 'church teaching' which might be expected to influence a Christian emperor. The formation of Church discipline was in many ways like the formation of Roman law. When a pastoral problem arose, a bishop or synod of bishops might be asked for a *canōn* —literally a 'rule', as in ruling a line—just as an emperor or a governor might be asked for a rescript. The canon was in principle binding on the Church in the relevant area; in practice, it depended on who got to hear about it. There was no coherent and generally accepted Canon Law available for consultation, and Church discipline varied over time and place, just as secular law did. Three of Basil's letters acquired canonical status,[3] but the codification of canon law probably did not begin (Macrides 1990) until 545, when Justinian decreed that the canons of the four great councils—Nicaea, Constantinople, Ephesus, and Chalcedon—had the status of law. The first *nomocanōn*, which integrates Church and secular rulings on matters concerning the Church, appears later in the sixth century.

We might suppose that people at least knew what the secular law was, but this cannot be taken for granted. Laws were often re-enacted, with greater indignation but little or no change in content: this suggests that they were less than effective. If there is an order to publicize—by proclamation or by putting up notices—demands that 'This Must Stop', we may reasonably suspect that it will not reach all the population (especially those in the country) and that the imperial power has no clear idea what is to be done about it. Local magistrates must, in practice, have had considerable discretion in applying the law.

---

[3] These are *Letter* 188 (canons 1–16; PG 32. 664–84), *Letter* 199 (canons 17–50; PG 32. 716–32), and *Letter* 217 (canons 51–84; PG 32. 792–809).

We cannot, then, assume either that people in general knew what exactly the law was, or that law gives information on general behaviour and social attitudes. This does not mean that late Roman law is useless to us. A full survey of laws affecting women would take another book.[4] The rest of this chapter, and the next, offer some examples of what law can tell us about the general conditions under which women lived, what they were thought to be like, how they were protected or restricted, and how opinions differed.

1.2. Arranging a Marriage

Any woman, it was assumed, wanted to marry and have children. 'Nature produced women for this very purpose, that they might bear children, and this is their greatest desire' (Justinian, CJ 6. 40. 2, AD 531). A woman might be unable to marry because of her low social status or because her family could not give her a dowry; she might make the heroic choice not to marry in order to devote herself to God (and this commitment was seen as a kind of marriage, making her the bride of Christ); but marriage or its absence was still the central fact of her life. She did not have the option of a career or profession. Her dowry was, in all probability, the biggest financial transaction in which she was ever involved, and it was certainly a major investment by her family: often (though not always: Saller 1984) it was her share of the family inheritance.

Because marriages were so important, they were arranged early, by the girl's family or guardian. They were not left to the free choice of the marriage-partners, who might well not meet until the marriage was decided. Thus John Chrysostom suggests to Christian fathers a tactic for keeping adolescent sons on the path of virtue: 'Promise him too that you will lead him to a lovely girl, and tell him that you have made him the heir of your property' (*On Vainglory* 61; Laistner 1951: 111). The earliest legal age for a formal betrothal was seven (D. 23.

---

[4] For more extended treatments, see Beaucamp (1977, 1990) for the eastern empire; Arjava (forthcoming), especially for the western empire and its successors. Robinson (1987*a*, 1987*b*) sets late Roman law on women in the context of classical law.

1. 14), when the parties were assumed to understand what was happening and could give formal consent. The earliest age for a legally valid marriage was 12, and most girls were married by 16; a father or guardian who had failed to arrange a marriage by then was suspected of political or financial scheming.

Formal betrothal was symbolized by a handclasp (*dextrarum iunctio*) and a kiss; the bridegroom sent his future bride a ring and other gifts (Treggiari 1991: 151–2). Betrothal was a serious financial commitment. Constantine ruled (CT 3. 5. 2, AD 319) that there was no such thing as a conditional betrothal gift: if the groom broke the engagement, the bride could keep his gifts and demand the return of hers (and vice versa). A law of 380 (CT 3. 5. 11) made the commitment binding when the girl was 10, and penalties for breaking off the betrothal increased as she reached her eleventh birthday. The fiancé of Macrina, sister of Gregory of Nyssa, died when she was 12; she declared that her betrothal was equivalent to marriage, and claimed the support of Christian tradition in refusing a second marriage (*Life of Macrina* 5, PG 46. 494). This was an extreme case, but understandable in terms of the importance of betrothal.

The essential factor in marriage was the consent of the parties. Usually, this consent followed on careful financial arrangements which were set down in a contract. The marriage was marked by the reading of the contract in the presence of witnesses, a party for friends and relatives, and the transfer of the bride to her new home, which also fixed the event in the memory of the neighbours. Both men and women might wear marriage rings (examples in Vikan 1990). Christian families liked to ask their priest to pronounce a blessing, or to set the 'marriage crowns' on the heads of bride and groom, but this did not amount to a religious as distinct from a civil marriage (Meyendorff 1990: 104–5).

Even where there was no money or property to assign, no documentation and no ceremony, friends and neighbours could attest that a couple considered themselves, and were considered by others, to be married. This did not mean that a man and woman could simply decide to be married (Beaucamp 1990: 239–55). Under Roman law, a child was in the *potestas*—that is power to take actions which have an effect in law—of his or her father until the father died; so the child could not independently contract a valid marriage. In the words of Basil of Caesarea, 'marriage without the consent of the power-holders is fornication' (*Letter* 199. 42, PG 32. 729). A girl could refuse to marry the man her father chose only if he was unworthy in status or behaviour (D. 23. 1. 11–12), and the choice of a dead father took precedence over that of mother, guardian or other kin—or the girl herself (CT 3. 5. 12, AD 422), since she might act against her own best interest. It was, after all, her father's property that she inherited. But the point is not simply financial. The father's headship of his household, formalized in Roman law as *patria potestas*, was a basic social fact, and it was assumed that he would do what was best for his children (Shaw 1987): a father would naturally wish to ensure that his daughter was properly treated by her husband. A woman remained in the *potestas* of her father, not of her husband, when she married, and became legally independent on her father's death. For almost all legal purposes, the import-ant question was not whether she was married, but whether she was still in *potestas*. If her father died when she was still young enough to need a guardian, she could apply at 18 to manage her own affairs. Until 25 she had some legal protection because of presumed inexperience (this also applied to young men), and, according to a law of 371 (CT 3. 7. 1), a widow under 25 who wished to remarry needed the consent of her father, or, if he had died, must negotiate with her kin. It had once been Roman practice that a woman whose father had died should have, even in adulthood, a guardian whose consent was required for major financial transactions affecting family prop-erty. But this 'guardianship of women' (*tutela mulierum*) had been steadily eroded and was obsolete by the fourth century (Dixon 1984: 348), as was the form of marriage which had transferred a woman from the *potestas* of her father to the control (*manus*) of her husband.

Security for women

The wife's financial security was very carefully protected. Any property she inherited or acquired after her father's death remained her own. Her dowry could be used by the husband from the time of marriage, but with the powerful restraint that he might have to give some or all of it back if there was a divorce—exactly how much depended on the law of the time and the terms of the marriage settlement. It did not simply become his property, even though he was more likely than his wife to engage in whatever business supported the family (Treggiari 1991: ch. 10). 'This property was the wife's from the outset, and naturally remains in her ownership: the truth of the matter is not eliminated or obscured by the legal subtlety which makes it appear part of the husband's estate' (CJ 5. 12. 30, AD 529). If the husband had a financial disaster, return of dowry took precedence over the claims of his creditors.

We are aware of the absurdity that some women, who do not behave well, have an income from their bodies and live off that; whereas others, who have been properly brought up, entrust themselves and their property to a husband, and not only have no income if he does badly, but actually lose out . . . We know the weakness of female nature, and we understand very well how easily they are defrauded. We do not allow their dowry to be diminished in any way. (*Nov.* J. 97. 3, AD 539)

This was a sympathetic restatement of a traditional principle. 'Dowry cases take precedence always and everywhere, for it is in the public interest that dowries be safeguarded for women: it is absolutely essential that women should be dowered to procreate offspring and replenish the state whith children' (D. 24. 3. 1).

Dowry, which might look to us like a bribe to an intending husband, was in fact intended to give a wife status and security independent of her husband. Bride-price, which might seem to acknowledge her value, would have left her in her husband's power. The point is made in Justinian's outspoken disapproval of the Armenians, who would have to mend their ways now that they were part of the Roman empire: they must end

inheritance by men, but not women, from parents and brothers and other relatives, as is their barbarian custom; and, which is still more barbaric, their present custom which gives women to husbands without a dowry and lets them be bought by their intending partners.

They are not the only ones who think in this savage fashion; other peoples also dishonour nature thus and do violence to the female sex, as if it did not originate from God and contribute to the work of generation, but was something cheap, disregarded, and deserving to be excluded from all honour. (*Nov. J.* 21, AD 536)

A wife was not allowed to give her husband money or property: it was a traditional principle of Roman law that gifts could not be made between husband and wife, because love or pretended love (what Constantine called the 'usually deceptive blandishments' of spouses: CT 8. 16. 1, AD 320), could lead to financial loss. The one exception to this rule was a further security for married women, the 'nuptial donation' (Katzoff 1985). This was a gift (or designation) of money or property by the bridegroom to his bride, and could be paid after the marriage had taken place. This practice was eastern, not Roman, in origin, but spread rapidly. Nuptial donations rose in value, and by the time of Justinian (*Nov. J.* 97, AD 539), it was expected that the donation should be equal in value to the dowry, so that both parties should profit equally from the marriage.

If the marriage ended by a divorce she had not provoked, or by her husband's death, the woman retained the donation as well as the dowry (with legal restrictions on what she might keep if she remarried). That is, if the property was still there to retain, and if the woman was able to claim the dignity and independence which the aristocratic law-makers sought to give her: as John Chrysostom pointed out (*Against Remarriage* 5, PG 48. 616), a powerful husband could simply constrain his wife. Augustine, and (it seems) his congregation in a small North African town, accepted his mother's opinion that the marriage contract made wives the slaves of their husbands, and they should accept the fact (Shaw 1987).

1.3. Divorce and Remarriage

Could a woman escape from a marriage she wanted to end? In classical Roman law, the answer was certainly 'yes', provided she had the financial and moral support of her family, or was legally independent. The law allowed both divorce by mutual consent and unilateral divorce, and scholars writing before the twentieth-century reforms of English divorce law tend to see it as very civilized. There was no need for a legal dispute unless there were financial problems; the chief concern of the law was to redistribute the property of the couple fairly with regard to blame and to the interests of the children. Divorce was a fact of life, made necessary by infertility, misconduct, or (less often) incompatibility, or used in political and economic manœuvres for the good of the natal family. It was stressful, financially if not otherwise, and potentially scandalous, especially when a woman sought to repudiate her husband, but it was not unthinkable. Marriage was a contract made by people, which could therefore be unmade by people; the children had to be considered, but with regard to their inheritance, not the far more difficult problem of their emotional security.[5]

Most people assumed that a divorced, or widowed, woman would seek to remarry, unless she refrained in the interests of her children. The law set no limits on what is now called 'serial monogamy', the number of times a man or woman could remarry after the death or divorce of a spouse, unless a ban on remarriage was part of a penalty for provoking divorce (see below). The concern of the law was not to prevent remarriage (Humbert 1972: ch. 2), but to ensure that the children's inheritance was not damaged by a dishonest or careless stepfather, or by their mother's rejecting them in favour of her new family. It may seem improbable that she should do this, but the expectation was that a woman's new family ties would replace the old—even if she was not divorced but widowed, and even if (whether divorced or widowed) she kept the children of her first marriage with her.

Children remained in the *potestas*, the legal power, of a divorced father, but did not necessarily live with him; if the father died before they were of age, their guardian had a say in where they lived. There is no question of the children making a choice: they were expected to obey the wishes of their parents,

---

[5] For classical law on divorce, see Gardner (1986) and Treggiari (1991); for late antiquity, Bagnall (1987), Evans-Grubbs (1987), and especially Arjava (1988). Christian teaching is discussed by Crouzel (1971, 1982), and the evolution of Augustine's thought by Berrouard (1972).

and in any prosperous household they spent more time with nurses and tutors than with their parents.[6] Maintenance could cause problems, as Justinian realized (*Nov.* J. 117. 7, AD 542). His solution was for the children to live with the parent who had not provoked the divorce, maintained at the expense of the father; but if the mother was richer, she had to raise the children.

A woman was expected to leave her property with due regard for all her children, even if she had remarried and had a second family, and this expectation was eventually formalized in law (Y. Thomas 1991: 123). Strictly speaking, a woman had no rightful heirs because there was no one in her *potestas*: until the late second century AD, if she died intestate it was not her children, but her father or her kin, who would inherit. So the good mother made a will and left her property to her children, unless she had reason not to. A ruling of 321 (CT 2. 19. 2) allowed children to complain of an 'undutiful will' if they had not inherited at least a quarter of their mother's estate (provided they could show that they had not been undutiful to her). A woman who remarried was forbidden to give or promise her new husband an 'undutiful dowry', that is, one large enough to deny her children their quarter share (CT 2. 21, AD 358); and when she died the children of her previous marriage inherited everything she had acquired from their father, including the nuptial donation. A mother who had behaved to her son as if she were his enemy (CJ 3. 28. 28, AD 321—a fine piece of Constantinian invective) could not claim that his will was undutiful in neglecting her.

A woman who married once and for life was admired as *univira*, a 'one-man woman', but there was no point in censuring a woman who remarried unless she behaved badly to her children. A few aristocratic families prided themselves on not divorcing, and a few traditional Roman cults had required indissoluble marriage, or had given special status to the *univira*, but this does not imply any general religious principle against remarriage (Lightman and Zeisel 1977); and Greek tradition seems scarcely interested. The special cultic status of the *univira*

---

[6] For recent studies of child-care at Rome, see Dixon (1988), Wiedemann (1989), Bradley (1991).

is like that of children with both parents living: she is an instance of good fortune, not of merit. Remarriage might, of course, bring social problems: John Chrysostom (*On Virginity* 37, PG 48. 559) says that second marriages, though permitted by the law, provoked unpleasant gossip, not to mention troubles with stepdaughters and with the memory of the first wife. But remarriage might still seem preferable to life as a widow or divorcee with social and financial problems.

Roman tradition on divorce and remarriage was very different from Christian teaching. This rested on Jesus' response (Matt. 19: 3–9) to a question whether it was permitted, in Jewish law, to divorce a wife for any and every reason. (The exact wording of Matt. 5: 32, which also discusses divorce, and of Matt. 19: 9, differed in Biblical texts: see Crouzel (1971) for the variants.) Jesus rejected divorce except for fornication—the 'Matthaean exception'—on the grounds that people should not separate those whom God has joined. The parallel passage in Mark 10. 2–12 offers no exception, but it was generally assumed that Matthew gave the fuller version, not that the original teaching had been softened. This was not special pleading: it is characteristic of patristic exegesis to suppose that the fullest version is the best. Paul, writing in the middle of the first century to the Church at Corinth (1 Cor. 7: 10–16), reaffirmed as Jesus' command that a woman should not separate from her husband—and if she does, she must not remarry—and a man should not divorce his wife. On his own authority, he said that a Christian married to a non-Christian might separate if the unbelieving spouse wished it (the 'Pauline privilege'), although it was better to remain married in the hope of saving the partner. A letter to the Church at Ephesus, usually ascribed to Paul, added the powerful image that human marriage symbolizes the union of Christ and the Church. Consequently, a second marriage after the death of a spouse (sometimes called 'digamy') was a vexed question. Basil, and Gregory of Nazianzus, decided (Oikonomides 1976) that a second marriage could be tolerated; third and further marriages, even if the second spouse had died too, were not. 'The first is law, the second is concession, the third is unlawfulness, and anything after that is swinish' (Gregory of Nazianzus, *Oration* 37. 8, PG 36. 292).

Christians, faced with this divergence between the law of the State and the teaching of the Church, could proceed as they were generally advised to do in the later empire. The law of the State no longer required them to do things (for instance, sacrifice to pagan deities) which were forbidden by their religion, but it did tolerate conduct (for instance, divorce, prostitution, exposure of children) which was not acceptable for Christians. Christians must, therefore, live by a higher standard than human law: in this instance, they should refrain from divorce but concede it to a non-Christian partner, who might then remarry although the Christian would not. But the Church had, as always, to work out exactly what these teachings implied—for instance, whether a man could remarry after divorcing an adulterous wife—and to develop a pastoral response to those who had not met the standard (for the range of practice, see Meyendorff 1990: 101); and Christian emperors had to decide what the standards of human law should be in a far-from-Christian empire. Their efforts to do this shed a lurid light on late-antique marriage.

1.4. Divorce Law

In 331 (CT 3. 16. 1) Constantine issued a law on divorce which was probably a major change (we do not know for certain whether the classical law on divorce had been modified earlier). In impassioned Constantinian style (his own, or that of his advisers?), the new law declares:

A woman is not permitted to send notice of divorce to her husband, because of her depraved desires, for a far-fetched reason, as that he is a drinker or gambler or womanizer, nor are husbands allowed to divorce their wives for any and every reason. But when a woman sends notice of divorce, only the following charges shall be investigated: has she proved that he is a murderer, sorcerer, or destroyer of tombs? If so, she is praised and recovers her entire dowry. If she has sent notice of divorce for other reasons than these three charges, she should leave even her last hairpin in her husband's house and be deported to an island for her great presumption. If males send notice of divorce, these three charges shall be investigated: do they wish to repudiate an adulteress, a sorceress [*medicamentaria*], or a procuress? If a man expels a wife who is free from these charges, he must give back all the dowry and not marry another. If he does, the former wife shall be allowed to enter his house and transfer to herself all the dowry of the second wife, in compensation for the injury done her. (CT 3. 16. 1)

It is disconcerting to see that only 'depraved desires' could make a woman seek to divorce her husband for extramarital affairs, alcohol abuse, or gambling, all of which (leaving aside her own feelings) could do serious damage to family property and put her and her children at risk (see Shaw 1987: 31 for alcohol-related violence). But Constantine probably spoke for much late Roman public opinion in seeing these as ordinary faults in a husband, and in distinguishing between husband's and wife's extramarital sexual activities. Nevertheless, the law is an extraordinary piece of drafting. Adultery, homicide, and magic were capital crimes which had to be denounced and could not be amnestied, but they were by no means the only ones (MacMullen 1986b: 157). A *medicamentaria* (the Latin equivalent of the Greek *pharmakeutria*) used suspect drugs and perhaps spells, but her purpose might be anything from murder to abortion to the treatment of infertility or unrequited love (see below, Sect. 3.5). Moreover, the penalties are unclear. What exactly happens to property which is neither in the dowry, nor part of the marital home? And, most important of all, does the law refer only to unilateral divorce, the sending of a notice of *repudium*, or does it imply the end of divorce by mutual consent?

We do not know Constantine's purpose. As a Christian emperor, addressing the Christian prefect Ablabius, he might seek to put an end to 'easy divorce', particularly if Ablabius had recently had to deal with some frivolous divorces. When the pagan emperor Julian modified the law, probably in 363, we are told that women abused their new freedom: 'Before Julian's edict, women could not divorce their husbands; but when he came to power they began to do what previously they could not do: they began to divorce their husbands as they pleased [*licenter*] every day.' (Ambrosiaster, *Questions on the Old Testament and the New Testament* 115. 12, PL 35. 2348–9).

This late fourth-century Christian writer (known as Ambrosiaster because his works were formerly attributed to Ambrose of Milan: Hunter 1989: 284–7), over-simplified Constantine's law and probably did the same for Julian's. Julian may have returned to the classical law which aimed only to regulate the financial problems of divorce: he is known to have reaffirmed classical principles on the retention of dowry (CT 3. 13. 2, AD 363). If so, there might well be divorces 'every day' by women who had endured under Constantine's law. But their freedom did not last long.

By 421 (CT 3. 16. 2) the Constantinian penalties were (back?) in operation, but modified. It had to be clear that a woman who wanted a divorce was not seeking it only for the disgraceful reason that she wanted to marry someone else. A sliding scale of penalties tells us what she was expected to put up with. If she has no grounds for divorce, she loses dowry and nuptial gifts, is deported, and may not remarry. If she complains of 'flaws of character and ordinary faults'—we are not told what these may be—she is not actually deported. If she can prove serious crimes (again unspecified), she may keep the dowry and gifts, and may remarry, but after a five-year interval to make it clear that she divorced 'from loathing of her own husband rather than from a desire for another husband'.

The law is not, of course, symmetrical. If a man divorces his wife without grounds, she does indeed retain her dowry and gifts and may remarry after a year, whereas he may not. (The year's delay, which appears in other laws, is to allow time for the birth of any heir of the former husband: *Nov.* J. 22. 6. AD 535.) But if it is a question of character, not of crime, a husband who divorces gets off much more lightly. This time we know what faults are in question: the later Interpretation of the law specifies 'if, as often happens, the woman fails to please because of the frivolity of her character'. ('Suppose a husband is moderate, but his wife is wicked, critical, garrulous, extravagant—the usual fault of women': John Chrysostom, *On Virginity* 40, PG 48. 562.) He loses the dowry but not the nuptial gifts, and may remarry after two years. If there are serious crimes (unspecified), he must prosecute, and he acquires dowry, gifts, and the right to remarry at once. We still do not know whether divorce by consent was allowed.

Theodosius II, who had (in theory) approved this law, changed his mind twice. His first attempt was a return to classical law, aiming at the financial security of the children (*Nov. Th.* 12, AD 439): for this reason, he said, divorce could not be by consent, but there must be a formal notice (*repudium*). This law was not published in the western empire until 449; a year later Theodosius reverted to a distinction between justified and unjustified divorce (CJ 5. 17. 8). Perhaps there had been some hard cases. He allowed more grounds for justified divorce than in previous law. The list of crimes is longer, and a woman's grounds now included her husband's blatant infidelity: 'intercourse with unchaste women, in contempt of his home, before her very eyes, which particularly enrages chaste women.' Marital violence likewise allowed the wife to recover her dowry and remarry after a year. A man's grounds included his wife's insistence on going, against his wishes or without his knowledge, to the circus, theatre, or arena. Such places were unsuitable at best and dangerous at worst: Justinian (*Nov. J.* 22. 15, AD 535) specified plays and contests between men and beasts (MacMullen 1986a: 329) as unacceptable, and Procopius observed (*Wars* 1. 24. 6) that women who had not been able to watch the Blue and Green teams in the chariot races at Constantinople joined in the riots started by their supporters. Going to parties with men who were not kinsfolk, or staying out overnight without good reason, were also barred: such things would have cast doubt on the woman's chastity. A woman who divorced without grounds lost dowry and gifts and had to wait five years to remarry; a man who divorced without good reason merely lost dowry and gifts.

The law on divorce continued to be modified, with a frequency which suggests strong feeling and great divergence of views. Shortly after the death of Theodosius II, his law of 449 was abrogated in favour of a return to the law of 421 (*Nov. Val.* 35. 11, AD 452). This meant fewer grounds for justified divorce, and perhaps also (Bagnall 1987: 45) that divorce by consent was disallowed in the western empire; in the eastern empire it was allowed, and in 497 Anastasius reduced the five-year wait to one year if a groundless divorce was by consent (CJ 5. 17. 9). Justinian at first maintained the principle of divorce by consent and added new grounds for justifiable divorce. A wife could divorce if her husband had been impotent for two years (CJ 5. 17. 10–11, AD 528): a later emendation (*Nov.* J. 22. 6, AD 535) makes it three years, because there had been cases of men who were able to beget children after two years' impotence. A husband could divorce because his wife had tried to procure an abortion; had gone bathing, out of lust, with other men; or had sought another marriage while still married to him. These grounds are said to come from older laws. Much of a later emendation (*Nov.* J. 22, AD 535) collects and revises legislation on marriage: it affirms the principles that marriage is made by the intention of the parties (not by dowry) and that any tie made by people can be loosed by people. There is no suggestion that divorce or remarriage is contrary to Christian teaching. Should either party decide (as Christians might) to lead a life of chastity, he or she counts as dead with regard to marriage, and the financial agreements for death come into force.

But later Justinian made drastic changes in divorce law. According to his successor Justin (*Nov.* Justin 140, AD 566), he thought in terms of his own strong-mindedness rather than other people's weakness. In 542 (*Nov.* J. 117. 8–9) he restated the grounds for unilateral divorce. A man could now be divorced for persisting in staying, after warnings, with another woman in the same city: this would imply that he was treating her as a concubine, which was not permitted while he had a wife. Wife-beating, which was taken for granted in Augustine's home town (*Confessions* 9. 9, PL 32. 772) was not one of the grounds for divorce, but carried a heavy financial penalty (*Nov.* J. 117. 14). Divorce by consent was banned except (ibid. 12) when there was an agreement to enter the monastic life. A woman who repudiated her husband without grounds (ibid. 13) was sent to a convent. Since Justinian thought it wrong (*Nov.* J. 127. 4, AD 548) to have different penalties for men and women, a later law (*Nov.* J. 134. 11, AD 556) provided that a man who repudiated his wife without grounds was sent to a monastery, and even a couple who had agreed to divorce without grounds were sent to a convent and a monastery respectively. These laws were duly repealed by Justin II (*Nov.* Justin 140, AD 566), who observed that people do, unfortunately, have unhappy marriages without formal grounds for divorce. He therefore returned to ancient law and allowed divorce by consent.

What are we to make of this extraordinary sequence of restriction and concession? Should we conclude that emperors, on Christian principle, tried to make it more difficult to divorce, but were repeatedly frustrated by the hardness of heart of their subjects, or perhaps by their insistence that traditional freedom to divorce should continue? That is not what was said at the time. Christian clergy said that human law fails to meet Christian moral standards, and Christians should not think themselves entitled to live by it. Christian emperors did not claim to be legislating in accordance with Christian principle. Justinian's prefaces to the Digest invoke God's help for the massive task, but Justinian does not express an intention to rewrite the law in accordance with Christian teaching. To explain specific changes in the law, he sometimes invokes Roman (not Christian) tradition against barbarian custom, and he appeals to the rule of God and the facts of Nature (Maas 1986), but the most frequent explanation for a change is that the existing law was unclear or unfair. But, of course, it is too simple to say that laws were made by Christian emperors. Some jurists (notably Tribonian) were not Christian, even though they served a Christian emperor; traditional Roman law had been made for a non-Christian population and law still had to be applicable to non-Christians.

Divorce law, even at its most restrictive, failed to match the strictness of Christian teaching. Basil of Caesarea concluded, though with some unease, that Church tradition does not allow a wife to repudiate her husband for any reason at all (*Letter* 188. 9, PG 32. 677; see below, Sect. 2.4). Augustine decided (*On the Good of Marriage* 7, PL 40. 378) that even a man who divorces his wife for adultery, which disrupts the existing marriage, is forbidden to remarry before her death. Jerome affirmed the same principle for a woman who leaves her husband. 'So long as the man lives, even though he is an adulterer, a sodomite, covered with all kinds of wickedness and deserted by his wife because of his crimes, he is still held to be her husband, because she may not marry another' (*Letter* 55. 3, PL 22. 563). The Council of Carthage in 407 felt justified in requesting legislation to prevent the remarriage even of a deserted spouse (CCL 149. 218), but did not get it.

Perhaps we should conclude, on the one hand, that classical divorce law would have remained unchanged had there been no Christian emperors, but, on the other, that a non-Christian, or nominally Christian, population could not have been made to live by strict Christian teaching. Christian principle was not the only factor in legal change: others were the generally accepted standards of decent behaviour, especially by women, which are revealed in the grounds for justified divorce; the need to protect natal families, children, and the marriage-partners themselves in one of the major financial transactions of a lifetime; and the normal determination of human beings not to continue in a marriage they dislike. But, as divorce law in the twentieth century confirms, someone was always bound to suffer.

2

TOLERANCE, PROHIBITION, AND PROTECTION

THE State had to be concerned with the transmission of property in marriage, and therefore with the ending of marriage in divorce. It was also concerned with other aspects of women's experience. Women might produce children, outside or within marriage, whose claim to inherit was doubtful. They might be raped or seduced: this could wreck their chances of marriage or seriously reduce their fathers' power to choose a husband, or, if they were married already, make people wonder whether any of their children was legitimate. They might refuse marriage or remarriage and opt for celibacy; and they might, even if married, try to avoid giving their husbands children. Once again, these are not simply questions of economics, or even of patriarchal attempts to maintain control over women and property. Late Roman law often expresses concern for the perceived weakness of women, and seeks to protect them from physical and financial exploitation.

Extramarital relationships were particularly likely to cause problems. Graeco-Roman culture had always accepted some sexual relationships outside marriage. Some stable, non-marital relationships were not only socially accepted but acknowledged in law as concubinage. But there was one law for men and another for women. A man, even if married, could make use of prostitutes or slaves (of either sex) without penalty—unless the slave was not his own and the owner objected. His infidelity became a ground for divorce only if it threatened his wife's status as mistress of the house. But if a married or marriageable woman had an extramarital sexual relationship with a man, she and her partner were severely condemned, since any doubt about her chastity also cast doubt on the legitimacy of her children. (There was almost no mention of women with female sexual partners: see below, Sect. 3.7.) Consequently, a married woman was an adulteress if she had any male sexual partner other than her husband; whereas a man was an adulterer, whether or not he was himself married, only if his partner was a married woman.

Christian teaching required fidelity within marriage and chastity outside marriage for both sexes. Many pagan moralists agreed, arguing that sexual desire is damaging to the soul, and that it should be indulged only for the procreation of legitimate children. Women, they said, must obviously be chaste; men, being in all respects the stronger sex, should not yield to desires they expect women to resist. But the double standard of sexual morality continued among the less high-minded. Legislators made occasional reproaches, but the law was chiefly concerned to ensure that property went to the legitimate heirs.

2.1. Prostitutes and Actresses

Since there was no certainty about the father of a prostitute's children, there was no valid marriage with a prostitute, or with a woman in the entertainment business, which, then as now, shaded into prostitution. Actresses, like any woman on public view, were assumed to be available sexual partners. A law of Constantine (CT 9. 7. 1, AD 326) distinguished the landlady of a public house, who presumably could choose to lead a respectable life, from the barmaid, who, presumably could not. A man could not marry a barmaid, and if he had intercourse with her (or any other woman in that category), there could be no charge of unlawful sexual intercourse (*stuprum*), which applied only when the woman was marriageable or quasi-married as a concubine (Gardner 1986: 124). The others were 'those on whom *stuprum* is not committed'. It is not clear how they could have had any legal redress against rape, unless they could bring a charge of injury.

Christian emperors before Justinian made little effort to alter this situation (Beaucamp 1990: 121–32). Repeated laws (CT 15. 7) forbade actresses, or their daughters, to leave their profession unless they converted to Christianity, which would imply strict sexual morality thereafter. Perhaps, being no longer actresses, they could then marry: Justinian made it clear (*Nov. J.* 117. 6, AD 542) that they could. Having himself—notoriously—married an actress, with special legislation to overcome the social gulf, he declared that the law, like the mercy of God, recognizes the possibility of repentance: ex-actresses may wipe out the stain of their past lives (CJ 5. 4. 23, *c.* AD 530). When he sorted out the law on sexual offences (CJ 9. 13, AD 528), he made no mention of the category 'those on whom *stuprum* is not committed': penalties differed according to the social status of the woman, but a man could be executed for the abduction (*raptus*, see below) even of a woman slave. Someone would have to care enough to take legal action on her behalf, but at least it was possible.

Without supposing that Justinian, or his wife Theodora, personally drafted the relevant legislation, we may allow for Theodora's knowledge of the conditions of life for such women (Honoré 1978: 9–12). She may not have had all the experience asserted by the historian Procopius, who says (*Secret History* 9. 1–30) that from childhood to maturity she was on display to the people of Constantinople, near-naked and engaged in explicit sexual mime, and that she had many sexual connections but learned to frustrate pregnancy. Procopius disliked Theodora and enjoyed the rhetorical tradition on wicked women (Fisher 1978; Averil Cameron 1986: ch. 5). But Theodora probably knew of the poverty and ignorance which forced girls scarcely 10 years old into prostitution (*Nov. J.* 14. 1, AD 535), lured from their parents by promises of clothes and food. (It still happens, in countries where people are as poor as they were in the rural districts of Justinian's empire.) A total ban on prostitution (attempted by Leo I: CJ 11. 41. 7, *c.* AD 460) was obviously unworkable. Theodosius had made efforts (CT 15. 8. 2, AD 428) to stop fathers or owners profiting from the prostitution of their daughters or their slaves, and Justinian (*Nov. J.* 14. 1, AD 535) tried to stop women being forced or tricked into prostitution: some prostitutes had been forced to swear an oath, or to sign a contract, to work for a pimp, and believed that the law would enforce it. Justinian and Theodora converted a palace into a splendidly furnished convent for former prostitutes and named it Repentance (Procopius, *Buildings* 1. 9. 2–9); perhaps, again, we need not believe Procopius when he says (*Secret History* 17. 5–6) that some of them escaped by leaping from a height.

In Christian romance, which is quite informative about prostitution, the redeemed prostitute does not marry but goes to the other extreme, emulating the austerity of the ascetic whose non-sexual love has rescued her. Pelagia the harlot, first seen adorned with silks and jewels and riding a white mule, is redeemed by the prayers of an ascetic who realizes her true beauty of soul: she gives all her wealth to the Church and embarks on a life of self-mortification. Maria, niece of the ascetic Abraham, is seduced, and in her despair seeks work in a tavern which is in effect a brothel; redeemed by Abraham, who poses as a client, she returns to a life of renewed austerity. (Brock and Harvey 1987; Ward 1987.)

2.2. Concubines and Slaves

A concubine was emphatically not a prostitute: though unmarried, she was acknowledged as belonging to a particular man, so that her children could be assumed to be his. She and her children therefore had some claim on him, but they did not share his social status, and their moral claim to any share in his property had to allow for the rights of legitimate heirs. A man might choose to take a concubine, in preference to remarrying, precisely to avoid adding to the number of his heirs or giving his children a stepmother. It was also common for a young man to take a concubine who would be dismissed when he married.

Roman law had, in fact, some difficulty in distinguishing a (free) concubine from a wife (Treggiari 1981), since an agreement to live together, the woman remaining faithful to the man and the man willing to acknowledge her children, was precisely what made a marriage. Absence of dowry did not prove that there was no marriage, because poor families might be unable to give a dowry. So it had to be asked whether the couple had 'marital intent'—and what happened if one had and the other had not? In practice (Beaucamp 1990: 266) it was the man's intent that mattered. Sometimes the low social status of the woman made it very unlikely that a marriage was in question; more often, the concubine was actually a slave, or was in one of the categories of women who could not make a valid marriage. (See further Rousselle 1988: ch. 6; Beaucamp 1990: 296–307.)

Roman law did not accept that a man could have a concubine and a wife at the same time, but ordinary usage was less precise. 'Your wife has just one man: why do you want two women? You reply: My slave-woman is my concubine. Would you rather I seduced another man's wife, or ran to a public prostitute? Can't I do what I like in my own house?' (Augustine, *Sermon* 224. 3, PL 38. 1095). Greek tradition had been more flexible than Roman on the social status of the *pallakē* (who might be a perfectly respectable woman from a family too poor to dower her) and on whether it was possible to have a concubine at the same time as a wife. Even so, a wife, or her family, was very likely to object to any arrangement which might challenge her own status as the mother of the legitimate heirs.

Christian teaching could not accept concubinage, but pastoral response varied (see below); and Christian emperors had to deal with society as they found it. It is not clear that they made any attempt to discourage concubinage. When we find Constantine legislating (CJ 5. 26. 1, AD 326) that it is not permitted to have a wife and a concubine at the same time, we need not assume that his object was to end extramarital relationships: he was affirming a principle of Roman law which may have been neglected in the eastern empire. He gave permission for men who had not married their concubines to do so and legitimize the children; unfortunately, this law is known only from its reaffirmation in 477 (CJ 5. 27. 5), and its original context and scope are uncertain.

When a man did not marry his concubine—which was the more likely outcome, since there had been socially valid reasons for not marrying her in the first place—there was some attempt to give legal protection to her and her children (Beaucamp 1990: 195–201). In classical Roman law, a child born out of wedlock was not part of the father's family, and had no claim to inherit unless named by the father as an 'outside' heir. Post-classical law varied between allowing natural children a small proportion of the estate, and excluding them altogether, depending on what their father had done to acknowledge them (Wolff 1945). Justinian noted (*Nov.* J. 74. 5, AD 538) that there were men who would swear on the Gospels, or in church, to marry a woman, and then tire of her and throw her out. He listed in several laws (the fullest is *Nov.* J. 89, AD 539) the various methods for a man to legitimize children whose mother he had been unable or unwilling to marry. If the man had not made a will, Justinian allowed (*Nov.* J. 89. 4–5, AD 539) a concubine and her children to inherit part of the estate, but on very restricted conditions. It had to be established that there were no legitimate heirs, and that the man had regarded the woman as his concubine, living with her and taking responsibility for the children. If he had a wife, or other mistresses, the woman he had not married could not be regarded as a concubine.

It could, of course, happen that a woman of low social status had believed herself to be a wife but could not prove it. Here, Justinian ruled that, even if there is neither dowry nor documentation, 'marital intent' is what counts (*Nov.* J. 22. 18, AD 535). A concubine's children could also be disadvantaged if she went on to marry and have legitimate children: Justinian decided (CJ 6. 57. 5, AD 529) that if at the time of her concubinage she was free and the acknowledged partner of a free man, all her children could inherit from her. This did not apply to a woman of high social status (*illustris*), who had no need to accept concubinage. If she had legitimate children and also a child with an unknown father, the illegitimate child could not inherit from her, since such women are particularly bound to observe chastity.

Slaves

The barrier between slave and free—even if both were Christians and faithful to each other—remained insuperable. A slave could not marry because he or she had no rights over children or property, and was himself or herself in the power of an owner. Benevolent owners might recognize the partnership (*contubernium*) of their slaves, and refrain from separating slave families (Bradley 1991), but they retained their legal rights. The Theodosian Code (4. 12) collects legislation on the first-century *senatusconsultum Claudianum* (AD 52), which had provided that a free woman might cohabit with a slave if she had his owner's consent, and that the children (who would normally have taken the status of their mother) would be slaves; if the owner had not consented, the woman also lost her freedom. The obvious context for this measure is the great wealth and importance of some slaves in the household of the Roman emperor, which made them acceptable partners even though marriage was not possible. Bishop Callistus of Rome, in the mid-second century, probably had to deal with the same situation. He caused outrage by ruling that such cohabitations, though they were not marriages in law, need not be denounced as fornication.

What would a Christian emperor decide? The *senatusconsultum Claudianum* remained in force for two centuries with only minor modifications (Beaucamp 1990: 184–95). A law of 314 (CT 4. 12. 1), which was retrospective, allowed the woman to claim her rights if she had been forced to cohabit, but denied her and her children freedom 'if she has forgotten her dignity'. In 320 (CT 4. 12. 3) Constantine added that cohabitation with imperial slaves was different: the woman retained her free status, the children were free but without full rights of citizenship or inheritance, and there could be exemption for 'thoughtless mistake, simple ignorance, or a youthful lapse'. Eventually, Justinian ruled (CJ 7. 24. 1, *c.* AD 531) that respect for liberty made it unacceptable for a woman to lose her freedom in such circumstances. But he retained Constantine's ruling (CT 9.9 = CJ 9. 11, AD 326) that a woman who cohabited with her own slave was liable to capital punishment, and that anyone, even a slave, could denounce her. The emperor Anthemius (*Nov. Anth.* 1, AD 468) was petitioned by a woman who had freed her slave first (he had an excellent character) and then married him: she was not punished, but the emperor ruled that it was not to happen again. In less happy situations, the woman might have used force, threatening her slave with torture or death; but it seems to have been taken for granted that rapists and seducers were male.

2.3. Adultery, Abduction, and Seduction

The double standard ruled in late Roman law. As we have seen, a woman's adultery was grounds for divorce even under the most restricted law—though families might choose to condone it rather than cause a scandal or worse. Basil advised that an adulterous woman should be excluded from communion, but that the reason should not be made public 'lest we cause her death' (*Letter* 199. 34, PG 32. 728). Later canonists explained that he had in mind the danger of violence, not a death penalty, but the range of penalties for an adulterous woman does seem to have included a death sentence (see, further, Beaucamp 1990: 139–70). Constantine actually made it easier for families to turn a blind eye, by repealing the provision in the *lex Julia de adulteriis* (of Augustus, late first century BC) that if the woman's husband or father had failed to prosecute within a stated time, anyone might. Adultery, he said, was criminal, but a matter for close kin (CT 9. 7. 2, AD 326); it was not proper for outsiders to disturb a marriage.

A husband's infidelity, as we have also seen, was not taken seriously unless he threatened his wife's status by installing another woman in his house or spending most of his time in another woman's house, or if his affairs were so blatant as to insult his wife. But a man who seduced another man's wife had committed a most serious offence. The jurist Papinian (D. 48. 5. 6. 1) derived the word *adulterium* from the conception of another man's child; a married woman who had intercourse with another man cast doubt on her own past chastity, and therefore on the legitimacy of all her children. The execrable adulterer, said the ninth-century emperor Leo, is worse than many murderers: a murderer may take only one life, but the adulterer breaks the bonds of marriage and destroys the husband, his children, and their relatives.

Adultery therefore ranked as a major crime. Together with

sorcery and homicide, it was excluded from the amnesties declared on days of great celebration (such as Easter or the birth of a prince). Constantine's immediate successors declared that convicted adulterers should not be allowed to play for time with appeals: they should be sewn in a sack and burnt alive like parricides (CT 11. 36. 4, AD 339). We do not know whether they were, or whether the intention was to show how heinous a crime adultery was. Even an unsuccessful attempt to seduce a married woman could be punished (D. 47. 11. 1, 2); and it was an injury to her status (D. 47. 10. 1, 2) to remove her companion so that she was unaccompanied, and might be suspected of misconduct.

Abduction and seduction

The crime of *raptus* (Beaucamp 1990: 107–20) was also excluded from amnesties. This was not necessarily rape and did not necessarily imply sexual intercourse: *raptus*, like the eighteenth-century 'ravish', covered abduction, seduction, and rape. For us, the obvious question to ask is whether the woman was actually a rape victim, but late Roman law has other priorities. A girl or woman who was abducted, whether or not intercourse had taken place, had in any case lost her reputation and her chance of marriage to anyone except her abductor. Her family was thus left without a choice, so *raptus* was in fact a known tactic for making a family consent to a marriage, and the girl was not always a helpless victim (Evans-Grubbs 1989). This, not violence against women, is what provoked so much anger: just as adultery denied a husband his right to legitimate heirs, so *raptus* denied a father his right to choose the man who would benefit from his daughter's inheritance.

Constantine's law on *raptus* (CT 9. 24. 1, AD 320) is unusually dramatic even for him. He specifies that it makes no difference whether the woman claims she was overpowered or the abductor claims that she consented: she could have screamed for help, and if there was no one to hear her she should have been safely at home. If her parents fail to prosecute, in the hope of hushing things up, they are to be deported; informers are encouraged to come forward.

Accomplices are penalized according to their social status—by burning, if they are slaves; and if a slave nurse had assisted in the *raptus*, she was to have molten lead poured down her lying throat (so much for Romeo and Juliet). The penalties were so horrendous that people were reluctant to take action, and Constantius toned down the law (CT 9. 24. 2, AD 349). If the woman abducted or approached was dedicated to celibacy, whether virgin or widow, her consent to marry made (not surprisingly) no difference, and prosecution was not restricted to family members (CT 9. 25. 3, AD 420). Church councils (Payer 1984: 38) joined in the chorus of denunciation.

Justinian's law on *raptus* (CJ 9. 13, AD 528) is an important development. It covers the abduction, seductions or rape of all women, whether virgin, dedicated virgin, or married, free or slave. The category 'those on whom *stuprum* is not committed' does not occur. Once again, it is not asked whether the woman consented or whether rape has occurred—but, whereas Constantine's law assumed that the woman was at fault, Justinian's law shifts the blame, on the grounds that even a willing woman would have no scope for sinning if men did not try to make her do so.

Penalties for *raptus*, in Justinian's law, differed according to the social status of the woman, not the level of violence inflicted on her, or the social status of the man concerned. A *raptor* caught in the act might be killed by the kin or owner of the woman, especially if he had committed adultery—and even if the woman was his own betrothed, for marriages must be properly made. If the woman was a slave or freedwoman, the *raptor* was executed but his heirs might retain his property; if she was freeborn, she took his property and that of any accomplices, and might marry anyone she chose—except the *raptor*, who was executed. (Thirty years later, Justinian had to deal with a misunderstanding: *Nov.* J. 143, AD 563; people were acting under the impression that a woman who had married her *raptor*, in contravention of the law, should inherit his property in accordance with it.) What happened if she was an adulterous wife? She might, if her husband and family could face the scandal, be divorced and then prosecuted with her lover, but a later law of Justinian (*Nov.* J. 134. 10, AD 556) allowed the possibility of punishment followed by forgiveness: she should be corporally punished and should spend two years in a convent, where she would remain unless her husband decided to take her back.

2.4. *Christian Moral Standards*

It was an uphill task to reform the sexual morality of the Christian laity. Men continued to behave in ways which did not really seem to them (or their families) to be wrong. Caesarius of Arles observed (*Sermons* 42. 5, 43. 5) that, if he excommunicated all the men who had concubines, the Church would be seriously depleted. Salvian of Marseilles (*On the Government of God* 7. 4, PL 53. 133) thought the Vandals had the answer: they made prostitutes marry, so that their husbands would keep them from straying, and punished all extramarital affairs of men and women alike. In Salvian's opinion, even a man's intercourse with his household slaves reduced his wife's dominion over her household. But many Christian wives agreed with Graeco-Roman tradition: a good wife should pretend not to notice her husband's infidelity (which also, to be practical, might allow her to space pregnancies).

There are daily complaints, though women do not now dare to complain of their husbands. Custom has taken over and is observed as if it were law: men may do this, women may not. They hear of women dragged to the forum if they are found with slaves. They have never heard of a man dragged to the forum because he was found with a slave-woman. Yet the sin is equal. In equal sin, it is not God's truth but human perversity which makes the man seem more innocent. (Augustine, *Sermon* 9. 4, PL 38. 78)

Augustine very properly protested against the double standard, and, as Bishop of Hippo, exhorted wives to put up with everything but infidelity (*Sermon* 392. 4, PL 39. 1711). His mother, who had been a traditional wife (*Confessions* 9. 9, PL 32. 772), would probably have told him that his tactics were wrong, and more likely to provoke violence than to bring about reform.

A married man was urged to abandon any other sexual relationships; an unmarried man who had a mistress was not always urged to make an honest woman of her. Before his conversion, Augustine had himself lived for thirteen years with a concubine, from his undergraduate days at Carthage to his professorship of rhetoric at Milan. He was not yet married and did not want children, though he was devoted to the son born, not by their choice, in the first year of their relationship. When his mother urged him to marry, there was no question of his marrying his concubine rather than the girl his mother found for him. The concubine may not even have been capable of marriage, and was certainly of low status. The girl came of a good Christian family but—being only 10—was not available at once to marry the 30-year-old Augustine; her family would have been deeply offended if the concubine had remained. So the concubine returned to Africa and a celibate life, whereas Augustine promptly found a substitute (*Confessions* 6. 13–15, PL 32. 731–2). In later years he told his congregation that it was not acceptable to have a concubine before you married, and argued that a man who dismissed a faithful concubine, in order to marry, had committed adultery in his heart—not against his wife, but against his concubine, who was guiltless if she maintained her fidelity (*On the Good of Marriage* 5, PL 40. 376–7). The council of Toledo (AD 400) declined to excommunicate a man who lived faithfully with a concubine. But half a century later, Pope Leo (*Letter* 167, PL 54. 1205) ruled that a previous relationship with a concubine did not exclude marriage: this was not bigamy, but moral improvement (Crouzel 1982: 8).

The Church made repeated attempts to redefine adultery as infidelity by either spouse.

Just as we punish women who give themselves to others although they are married to us, so are we punished, if not by Roman laws, then by God. This too is adultery. The sexual act is adulterous not only when the woman is bound to another man: it is also adulterous for the man who is bound to a wife. Listen carefully! You may not like what I say, but I have to say it, to put you right for the future. (John Chrysostom, *Homily* 5 *on Thessalonians* 2, PG 62. 425)

But even the teachings of Jesus could be interpreted in accordance with all-powerful custom. In the system of penance

which can be deduced from Basil's letters, it took four years for
a fornicator to be reconciled to the Church (Basil, *Letter* 199.
22, PG 32. 721), fifteen for an adulterer (ibid. 217. 58, PG 32.
797), and seven for a man who abandoned his wife, though by
the Lord's teaching he was an adulterer (ibid. 217. 77, PG 32.
804). Presumably he had at least not disrupted another man's
marriage. Basil was also asked to rule on the question of a
woman who is living with a man to whom his wife had sent
notice of divorce, and produced a characteristically thoughtful
response:

The Lord's declaration about not leaving a marriage except for reason
of fornication, according to the implication of the thought, applies
equally to men and women. But custom differs from this, though on
the subject of women we find great precision: the Apostle says, 'he
who unites with a prostitute is one body', and Jeremiah says, 'if a
woman is with another man, she shall not return to her husband but
shall be defiled', and 'the man who keeps an adulteress is senseless and
irreligious'. But custom ordains that men who commit adultery or
fornication shall remain married. So I do not know whether the
woman who lives with the man who has been repudiated can be
called an adulteress. The charge in fact relates to the woman who
divorced her husband: what was her reason for leaving the marriage?
If she was beaten and did not bear the blows, she ought to have
endured rather than separate from her husband; or if she did not bear
financial loss, that too is not a valid reason. But if it was because he
lived in fornication, we have no provision for this in Church custom.
But a woman is not instructed to separate even from an unbelieving
husband, but to remain, because it is unclear what will result. 'Can
you know, wife, whether you will save your husband?' Thus the
woman who leaves her husband is an adulteress if she goes to another
man. But the man who is left is pardonable, and the woman who lives
with one such is not condemned. Nevertheless, if a man leaves his
wife and goes to another, he is himself an adulterer because he makes
her commit adultery; and the woman who lives with him is an adulteress, because she has transferred another woman's husband to
herself. (Basil, *Letter* 188. 9, PG 32. 677)

The movement of Basil's thought is not entirely clear, but
his argument appears to be as follows. If Jesus allows a man to
repudiate his wife for her fornication (and only for that reason),
then a woman should be able to repudiate her husband for

his. But Scripture does not say so, though it says a lot about women, nor does Church tradition. The emphasis of Church tradition is that a woman should not repudiate her husband at all. So, if the wife left her husband (and Basil is as illuminating as Roman divorce law on what she was expected to tolerate), it is pardonable that he is living with another woman: the Greek word Basil uses, *sunoikein*, could mean that in terms of ordinary social assumptions he has in fact married her. On the other hand, if the wife took up with another man, it would be adultery. The point is more bluntly made in another canonical letter (ibid. 199. 21, PG 32. 720). A married man who has intercourse with a divorcee is a fornicator, not an adulterer, and his wife should take him back; but a husband should expel a wife polluted by extra-marital intercourse. 'It is not easy to give a reason for this, but so custom has prevailed.'

2.5. 'A man may not marry . . .'

Some people were ruled out as marriage-partners because of their social status; others because they were close kin. *Stuprum*, unlawful intercourse, included *incestum*, intercourse with those too closely related. From an anthropologist's perspective, this is an important question, because the structure of the family is determined by rules on incest (that is, which kin count as too close to marry) and endogamy (a preference for marrying close kin). So any change in the rules has long-term consequences. There was very little disparity between traditional Roman attitudes and official Christian teaching on incest, but there was a recurrent problem about marriages which were acceptable by eastern standards and incestuous by western. Was it allowable for first cousins to marry, or for a man to marry his niece? If such marriages were classed as incestuous, it ruled out a favourite Greek and Eastern strategy for reuniting property which had had to be divided among heirs.

Roman tradition was generally hostile to cousin-marriage (Gardner 1986: 4–6), but a man's marriage to his brother's daughter had been legalized in the mid-first century for the benefit of the emperor Claudius. Church law, based on

Leviticus 18, interpreted the ban on incest as including both cousin-marriage and uncle–niece-marriage. Sometimes the Old Testament permitted or encouraged practices alien to Roman law, notably polygamy and the levirate (a man's marriage to the childless wife of his dead brother, to ensure offspring 'for' the brother); but these were classed as no longer appropriate (Manfredini 1988). Basil (*Letter* 160, PG 32. 622–8) explains that one must consider the social context of the Old Testament, the points it does not cover for reasons of modesty, and the extent to which Christians are bound by its law.

What, then, was the guiding principle on marriage partners? Augustine (*City of God* 15. 16, PL 41. 458) surveys the question with refreshing clarity. Ever since there were enough people in Adam's family, he says, the object has been to avoid linking the same two people in two different family relationships—for instance, uncle and niece who are also husband and wife—and to respect the sense of decency which recoils from the overlap of family affection and marital love. Particular laws have varied: for instance, legal prohibition of the marriage of first cousins is recent. But cousin-marriage was rare in any case, for the reasons given.

So far as we can tell, Augustine is right both on the general Roman feeling about marriage-partners, and on the particular case of cousin-marriages, at least in western Roman tradition (Shaw and Saller 1984). For permitted marriage-relationships, what mattered was the degree of kinship. This depended on the number of 'acts of generation' which brought about the relationship. Two 'acts of generation' are required to bring into being a brother and his sister, so they counted as kin in the second degree, whereas uncle and niece were kin in the third degree and first cousins in the fourth.[1] Roman law on degrees of kinship, which were important for inheritance on intestacy, was supposedly based on natural law (D. 23. 2. 14), that is on the kind of general human feeling invoked by Augustine. A law of Diocletian (CJ 5. 4. 17), issued at Damascus in 295, lists the prohibited kin in accordance with the opinion of the jurists Ulpian and Paulus. Marriage between ascendants and

---

[1] Degrees and terminology of kinship are listed in J. *Inst.* 3. 6; see further Goody (1983: 136).

descendants was not permitted (this applied even if the relationship was created by an adoption which was later cancelled), nor was marriage between kin in the 'third degree' with the one exception of a man's marriage to his brother's daughter (this is the 'Claudius' case). Marriage was also forbidden between a man and a woman who had been his stepmother, stepdaughter, daughter-in-law, or mother-in-law; and a law of 355 (CT 3. 12. 2) added his brother's ex-wife and the sister of a wife now divorced or dead.

So it is unlikely that there was much indignation in the western empire when Theodosius I passed the 'recent law' referred to by Augustine, forbidding the marriage of either *patrueles fratres* (children of two brothers) or *consobrini* (strictly speaking, children of two sisters, but increasingly a word for 'cousin' in general). According to one source (Aurelius Victor *Caesars* 48. 10), Theodosius banned marriage to a *consobrina* as to a sister: that is, the motive was a concern about incest. Greek and near eastern tradition, by contrast, saw such marriages as an expression of family loyalties. Worse, both Greeks and Romans believed that Persians indulged in clearly incestuous marriages between brother and sister or parent and child (H. Chadwick 1979; Lee 1988), and Roman subjects on the eastern frontiers of the empire were influenced by these practices.

We know about Theodosius' law from a letter of Ambrose (60. 8, PL 16. 1236) to one Paternus, who wishes to marry his son by one wife to the daughter of his daughter by another wife, and claims that the marriage is not forbidden by the Bible. Ambrose replies that the marriage of father and daughter is not forbidden by the Bible either, but is just as clearly wrong. Even though Paternus had two wives, the girl is still the niece of Paternus' son. This is kinship in the third degree, which is forbidden even by civil law; divine law forbids the marriage even of *patrueles fratres*, who are kin in the fourth degree, and Theodosius has banned the marriage of *patrueles fratres* and *consobrini*. Not that it would matter, for Ambrose's argument, if he had not: divine law is, as usual, stricter than human. But, for Ambrose, the emperor is clearly doing the right thing.

Half a century later, Theodoret, bishop of Cyrrhus, wrote

(*Letter* 8) to some notables of Zeugma, a town in his north Syrian diocese. Surely, he says, they know better than to betroth a daughter to her paternal uncle or to allow the marriage of cousins? It is forbidden by divine and by human law; some may seek to justify it by letters from the emperor, but let them fear the great Law-maker. 'Examine in yourselves what the nature of a family is: an uncle is the same as a father, a niece as a daughter. Persians may dare to do such things, but not Romans nurtured in the faith.' Once again, divine law is stricter than human, and Theodoret thinks poorly of human concessions. But human law had by now changed: cousin-marriage had been permitted again since 404 (CJ 5. 4. 19). Theodosius' ban did not last long.

It is quite possible that Theodosius, the consciously orthodox emperor, sought to reunite his western and eastern subjects under a Christian law, in this as in other respects. But we have to see his attempt not just in these terms, but in the context of a persistent Roman effort to end eastern endogamy. Diocletian's law of 295, issued at Damascus, had failed to make an impact in the remoter east. 'Letters from the emperor', like those Theodoret rejected, continued to authorize (just this once) marriages which were forbidden by law but which had happened. Arcadius and Honorius (CT 3. 12. 3, AD 396) ruled that there would be no punishment for marriage to a niece, first cousin, or brother's ex-wife, but that the marriage would not be valid—that is, the children would not inherit. Justinian denounced 'lawless marriages' (the word is *athemitoi*, which implies violation of divine law rather than simple illegality) in Osrhoene and Mesopotamia: he offered clemency for the present, but capital punishment and confiscation of property for future offenders (*Nov*. J. 154, AD 535/6). A generation later, in 566, Justin II was still offering clemency: he endorsed Justinian, but accepted that it was natural for the Euphrates provinces to follow Persian example (*Nov*. 3; Lee 1988: 404–5).

In other words, once again we have Christian emperors diverging on a legal change which is welcome to Christian bishops, and probably also to many non-Christians. This particular question may seem unimportant: all that happened was that the lives of some women were, presumably, affected by marriage to a more distant relative than their families had wished, and the family's plans for transmitting property had to be rethought. But there may be wider implications. One form of cousin-marriage, the marriage of 'cross-cousins', is often found in traditional, close-knit societies. In this pattern, a brother chooses his sister's husband and plays an important role in the upbringing of her son. (English 'uncle' derives from the Latin word for a maternal uncle, *avunculus*, which means 'little grandfather'.) In due course the sister's son marries the brother's daughter, thus reuniting family property which had been divided. It has been suggested (Patlagean 1977: 118–28) that these close family ties were revived in the uncertain political situation of the later empire, and prompted both the ban on cousin-marriage and Justinian's insistence (CJ 6. 58. 14, AD 531) that it is wrong to discriminate between paternal and maternal kin. But the pattern is visible (Shaw 1984: 458–62) only in isolated communities; and Justinian's professed motive for his ruling was, as so often, respect for Nature and concern that women should be treated fairly.

When the rights of consanguinity remain intact for the male sex, why do we offend against nature and detract from legitimate right? . . . Who would endure . . . that they should be punished only because they were born women, or that the innocent offspring should be oppressed by the fault (if fault it is) of the father? (CJ 6. 58. 14. 5)

The ban on cousin-marriage may also have had long-term consequences. There is an influential argument (Goody 1983) that it was one item in a deliberate Church policy of disrupting 'strategies of heirship' in the interests of the Church, and that this policy had the (unintended) effect of determining the characteristic European family structure. By discouraging adoption, remarriage, and concubinage, by urging celibacy and abstinence, even by encouraging mothers to breast-feed rather than use wet-nurses (with some effect on fertility: see below, Sect. 3.5), the Church, Goody argues, sought to reduce the number of natural heirs born to families; by objecting to cousin-marriage, and thus redefining incest, it reduced endogamy and attacked the wish to keep property 'in the family'. The overall aim was to divert property to the Church.

But reviewers have challenged Goody both in detail and in principle (Shaw and Saller 1984; Verdery 1988; Verdon 1988), arguing that he is wrong about the patterns of kinship which prevailed before the Church had official backing. They have also pointed out that the results of any such policy would be either unpredictable or (financially) undesirable, leaving the Church, for instance, with the task of supporting poor widows who were discouraged from finding another man to support them, or virgins whom their families had refused to dower. It might be argued too that a high-minded non-Christian couple, by adhering to the standard philosophic teaching on the control of desire and the merits of breast-feeding, were likely to reduce the number of legitimate and illegitimate children born to the husband. The lesson here is probably to look for the feeling which prompted a particular legal change rather than for the supposed grand strategy.

2.6. Child-bearing

Marriage was, by definition, a relationship for producing legitimate children, and Christian and non-Christian moralists agreed in disapproving of married persons who terminated a pregnancy or refused to rear a new-born child. They argued that people ought not to bring into being more children than they are prepared to rear, and that, if they do not want more children, the answer is abstinence: only prostitutes need to know about contraception. Women who attempted abortion were suspected either of vanity, because they did not want pregnancy to spoil their figures, or, worse, of trying to conceal the effects of adultery. If married couples agreed on contraception or abortion, it must be either to indulge their lust as if they were fornicators, or because they were unwilling to share their property among too many children.[2] Nobody advocated a woman's right to choose. Doctors advised on the medical termination of pregnancy, which might be necessary if the foetus was dead or the mother in danger, and a midwife's

[2] Augustine, *On Marriage and Desire* 1. 15. 17, PL 44. 423–4; Ambrose, *Hexaemeron* 5. 18. 58, PL 14. 243.

skill included recognizing which babies were too sickly to rear. But the only excuse for abandoning a healthy child was desperate poverty.

There is very little evidence (Patlagean 1977: 145–55) on the actual size of families and the frequency of births. Maternal and infant mortality, a high valuation of celibacy, and financial constraints on marriage must all have limited the number of children born, even without resort to deliberate family limitation; recent research (Riddle 1991) suggests that contraceptive medicine may have been reasonably effective. Legal constraints on limiting the size of families, whether by abortion or by the abandonment of children, were less severe than the judgement of the moralists. The earliest evidence we have for a criminal charge of abortion comes from the time of Septimius Severus, late in the second century AD; but the content of the charge was not straightforwardly the destruction of the unborn child. The Digest chapter on the *lex Cornelia de sicariis et veneficis*, 'on killing [with a weapon] and poisoning', includes a discussion of what counts as 'poison'. The answer is drugs intended to kill; but a woman was exiled for giving, without intent to kill, a drug 'for conception' (*ad conceptionem*) whose recipient died (D. 48. 8. 3). Whether it was a drug 'to deal with—i.e. frustrate —conception', or 'to stimulate conception' is unclear: it could, in practice, have been the same drug used for different purposes (see, further, Sect. 3.5). People who administered love-potions or abortifacients, even if without malice, were likewise punished because they had given a 'bad example' (D. 48. 19. 38. 5).

The criminal charge here is the death, or likely death, of the woman whose pregnancy was in question. The death of 'that which was to be born' was not an offence in law, since the foetus counted as part of the mother and had no separate legal existence (Gardner 1986: 158). But if a father had been deprived of an heir, that was another matter. 'Emperors Severus and Antoninus responded that a woman who deliberately aborted should be exiled for a time, for it appears unfitting that she should, with impunity, defraud her husband of children' (D. 47. 11. 4.) If there was no complaint from a concerned male parent (or from his family wanting a posthumous heir), and if the woman survived, there was no problem for the law. It might also be very difficult to prove attempted abortion, since pregnancies were notoriously risky and unstable. 'If it has been proved that a woman has done violence to her entrails so as to abort a pregnancy, she is to be exiled' (D. 48. 8. 8): perhaps the use of instruments could be proved, but the traditional methods of drugs and massage would be much less obvious.

Christian writers (Noonan 1970) condemned abortion, at any stage of the pregnancy, as parental cruelty and the destruction of life. The abandonment of a new-born child also counted as murder. 'The woman who gave birth on the road, and did not take care of the foetus, is liable to a charge of murder' (Basil, *Letter* 199. 33, PG 32. 727). But there might be special circumstances.

The woman who did not take care of the foetus on the road: if she neglected it when she could have saved it, or thought she could conceal a sin, or behaved in a bestial and inhuman fashion, she is to be judged as in a case of murder. But if she was unable to care for it, and the new-born died from solitude and lack of what was necessary, the mother may be pardoned. (ibid. 217. 52, PG 32. 796)

It may be important that Basil does not use the words for 'baby' (*brephos, paidion*) but the neutral 'that which was conceived' (*kuêma*) and 'that which was born' (*gennêthen*), even when he is arguing that the culpable death of the new-born is murder.

Legislation, even by Christian emperors, expressed disapproval of those who abandon their new-born children, but imposed no clear penalty. 'Exposure' is the standard modern term for the 'putting out' of a new-born who is not to be reared by the natal family. The child was not actually killed, but would die if not 'taken up' by some other person. A law forbidding exposure would probably have been unenforceable, and it is not clear that the attempt was ever made. One law (CT 9. 14. 1, AD 374) does declare the killing of an infant to be a capital crime; but exposure is not killing. One commentator in the Digest (D. 25. 3. 4) does say that 'killing' a child includes not only smothering, but exposure and refusal to rear: 'he who rejects and denies nurture, and he who exposes in public places to evoke the pity he does not feel' has in effect killed his child. But there is a specific context, namely whether parents who have divorced before the birth of a child are responsible for the child's upbringing. It seems more likely that another law of 394 (CJ 8. 51. 2) expresses the usual reaction. 'Each one should nourish his offspring: if he has decided to expose it, he shall be subject to the *animadversio* which has been decided.' What was the *animadversio*, the reprimand or punishment? Perhaps only the clause which follows, that the parent or owner who has exposed a child cannot subsequently reclaim it.

Most communities had well-known places where children were left: Justinian (*Nov. J.* 153, AD 541) was informed that the church in Thessalonica was such a place. Exposure was a widespread social problem in a society which lacked effective birth control and welfare provision. We have no adequate statistics for the ancient world, and it is difficult to tell from the evidence just how common it was for babies to be abandoned (Boswell 1989: 3–51). But for later centuries we do have figures (K. Thomas 1989). Romania in the Ceaucescu years of the 1980s, when contraception and abortion were unavailable and poverty was widespread, offers a distressingly likely comparison which is supported by the records of foundling hospitals in the early modern period. There probably were far more babies abandoned than there were would-be adoptive parents.

The ancient world had no state-supported orphanages and no adoption agencies: only private charity and local initiatives, encouraged by the Church. There are references to *brephotropheia* (Boswell 1989: 197), which may be homes for abandoned babies. But desperate, or even indifferent, parents or owners might simply avert their minds from the likely fate of an exposed child, which Christian writers (Boswell 1989: 157–79) hammer home: if the child survives cold, starvation, scavenging animals, a man may years later commit incest with a son or daughter reared as a slave prostitute. Here Christian emperors did try to do something. Constantine, soon after he came to power (CT 11. 27. 1, AD 315), instructed the prefect Ablabius (a fellow-Christian) to advertise help for impoverished parents so that they might avoid *parricidium*, the murder of close kin. Some years later (CT 11. 27. 2, AD 322) he issued further instructions for help, so that parents need not be driven by hunger to sell or pledge their children. But he did allow such sales (CT 4. 43. 2, AD 329), unlike Diocletian (ibid. 1, AD 294), who had followed the traditional principle that someone who was demonstrably born free cannot become a slave.

By 331 Constantine was instructing Ablabius (CT 5. 9. 1) that those who 'knowingly and of their own free will put out of their home new-born free or slave children' could not reclaim the child; the finder could raise the child as slave or free. This ruling was reaffirmed in 412, with the comment 'the child he has disregarded as it perishes, he cannot claim as his' (CT 5. 9. 2). Justinian (Boswell 1989: 189–94) agreed that the child could not be reclaimed, but added that all exposed children should have free status: their finders should not appear to have had mercenary motives for their human kindness, even if in fact they had (CJ 8. 51, AD 529). He also ruled that a child could not be taken as a slave, or a pledge, in settlement of a parent's debt.

These laws envisage the father's decision to sell or pledge a child, but the decision to abort or to expose, risking the death or enslavement of the child, might in practice rest with the mother. She could claim (with the help of her midwife and attendants) that she had miscarried or that her baby was still-born. Conversely, she might be able to substitute a foundling for a stillbirth, or even pretend to have given birth when she had not—a theme of traditional misogyny. It was, of course, an offence to substitute a false heir, and in special circumstances, where a posthumous child or the child of a divorced husband would have claims to property, the courts might order that a pregnant woman should be watched and inspected by mid-wives (Gardner 1986: 52). But, in general, child-bearing was an aspect of women's lives which was particularly difficult for the law to control.

2.7. Celibacy

In 320 Constantine repealed the legal penalties which Augustus, three centuries earlier, had imposed on men and women who failed to marry. His edict, addressed to the people, makes the most of it:

> Those who were classed by the old law as *caelibes* (unmarried) shall be freed from the looming terrors of the laws: let them live as if included among the married and supported by the treaty of matrimony: let all be equally able to inherit what they deserve. And let no one be classed as childless; the losses prescribed for this name shall do no harm. We think this also with regard to women, and we release all alike from the yoke imposed upon their necks by the commands of the law. (CT 8. 16. 1)

The Augustan inheritance laws, designed to encourage the upper classes to reproduce and to discourage legacy-hunting by persons of dubious ancestry, were hardly terrifying. Unmarried persons were forbidden to inherit, except from kin within the sixth degree, which is a very wide circle of kinship. But there had always been resentment, and Constantine was able to present his measures of 320 (which included a simplification of procedure for wills) as the removal of outdated and oppressive laws.

Constantine may not particularly have intended, as early as 320, to benefit those celibate Christians who had opted to devote their lives to the service of God; still less (Drijvers 1987: 253) to undermine the power of a father to insist on his daughter's marriage. But once Christianity had official support, the law had to come to terms with celibate women. We have to remember how extraordinary it was, in Graeco-Roman terms, for a woman to opt not to marry. There were a very few cults which required lengthy, or in practice lifelong, celibacy in their priestesses. The most famous example is the Vestal Virgins. Ambrose (*Letter* 18. 11-12, PL 16. 1016) enjoys pointing out how few of them there were—it was difficult to recruit seven —by comparison with the multitude of Christian virgins. (In Antioch alone, the Church supported three thousand virgins and widows, according to John Chrysostom: *Homily 66 on Matthew* 3, PG 58. 630.) There were also some celibate priestesses in Asia Minor, so that the doctor Soranus of Ephesus (see below, Sect. 3.3) was able to compare the health of celibate and non-celibate women, and conclude that celibates did better.

The Christian Church as a whole regarded celibacy as a lofty vocation, and supported quite young girls who opted for life-virginity as well as widows who chose not to remarry. Basil, in a canonical letter (*Letter* 199. 18, PG 32. 717), says the choice should not be made until 16 or 17 and after repeated testing, but his sister Macrina made her decision at the age of 12, when her fiancé died. Married women who wished to be celibate were told to reach agreement with their husbands, who might otherwise fall into sin. But such 'post-marital celibacy' (Hunter 1989: 294) was a common expectation. Sidonius (*Letter* 9. 6) rejoices that a young man who had an expensive mistress has now married: it would have been even better if he had opted for celibacy, but as he has not, his friends must pray that, after the birth of one or two children (at most), he will abstain from lawful pleasures as he now does from unlawful ones. As the restrained behaviour of the young couple (according to Sidonius) demonstrates the difference between honourable matrimony and lust, celibacy seems a likely outcome.

When Christianity was still an objectionable cult, the choice of celibacy might well cause family problems. Oppressive families and fiancés, who call in the local governor to force the reluctant heroine into marriage, are a favourite theme of Christian romance (Kraemer 1980). Once Christianity was official, the Church's problem was combining support for celibacy with deference to fathers. Ambrose (*On Virgins* 1. 65–6, PL 16. 218) tells the story of a young woman who invoked the protection of the altar. 'If your father had lived, would he have let you remain unmarried?' someone demanded. 'Perhaps he died so that I could make this choice,' she replied. The questioner died soon after, like others who tried to frustrate resolute Christian girls (see below, Sect. 4.5). It was much more difficult if the young woman was an heiress, who could wreck the prospects of a family line, first by refusing to marry and produce heirs, and secondly by taking her inheritance with her to the Church or distributing it to God's poor. There was a further problem if the woman concerned was not an inexperienced girl, but a widow refusing a second marriage, especially if her father was dead and she was legally independent. The law could not forbid the choice of celibacy: in fact,

Justinian went so far as to declare (CJ 1. 3. 54. 5, AD 534) that parents were not allowed to disinherit a son or daughter, even if they were still in *potestas*, for choosing to enter the religious life. But law-makers did feel entitled to surround celibacy with the same safeguards as applied to marriage: they sought to ensure that nobody was being cheated or pressured into financial loss.

The problems which could be caused by celibacy appear in spectacular fashion in the élite of Rome and Constantinople, in the late fourth and early fifth centuries. Both Basil (*Letter* 199. 18, PG 32. 719) and Jerome had encountered families who had dedicated a daughter to virginity simply to save on her dowry. On the other hand, there were women who, on their own initiative, took their share of the family fortune out of family control. Those we hear about were great ladies, but the same thing could occur on a lesser scale. The elder Melania, widowed at the age of 22, made conscientious provision for her surviving son and stayed in Rome until his career was established. Paulinus of Nola (*Letter* 29. 9, PL 61. 317) says 'she loved her child by neglecting him'. Then, in 374, she set sail to visit the monks of Egypt and the Holy Land. She distributed largesse and established a monastery of her own. Paula, mother of five, was widowed soon after she finally achieved a son: leaving behind the little boy, two married daughters, and one daughter who was ready for marriage, she too left for the East. She was accompanied by her unmarried daughter Eustochia (Jerome uses the pet-name Eustochium), who renounced her share of the inheritance and took a vow of virginity; and confirmed Soranus' opinion by long outliving her married sisters, none of whom successfully bore children. Paula, like Melania, ensured that her children had their rightful inheritance, but used her own fortune to distribute among the poor and to found a monastery. She died heavily in debt, and her debts, too, were inherited.

Melania's granddaughter, the younger Melania, was perhaps (E. A. Clark 1984: 90–2) her father's only heir. She was constrained to marry, aged 13, and have children; the children died, she and her husband (also heir to a fortune) pledged themselves to celibacy, and while still under age attempted to sell all they had and give it to the poor—apparently without giving first option to their closest relatives. Melania's biographer presents the opposition of their families as one more hurdle for the saints to overcome. They succeeded in giving to the poor and endowing churches and monasteries to the point that when they reached Jerusalem they had no money left, and (much to their delight) thought of enrolling themselves on the bishop's welfare list. The fatherless heiress Demetrias, supported by her mother and grandmother, chose virginity: she was given the property which would have been her dowry, and used it to fund church-building in Rome after the Gothic sack of 411. In Constantinople, Olympias (married at 18 and widowed twenty months later) refused to take as her second husband a relative of the emperor, devoting herself instead to the bishop John Chrysostom and to good works. She had great difficulty achieving her rightful control of her fortune, and at one time (E. A. Clark 1979: 129–30) was accused of 'disorderly' disposal of her inheritance and forbidden even to meet bishops.[3]

So it is hardly surprising that legislation appeared—or that it is not consistent, for there were divergent interests at work. A law of June 390 (CT 16. 2. 27) dealt with women who wished to enrol as deaconesses. This was the highest official status which the Church offered women, since it accepted the cultural assumption that women were not suited to positions of authority, or capable of giving instruction except to other women (see below, Sect. 5.2). The deaconess could, without scandal, instruct women in preparation for baptism and escort them during the ceremony. Olympias was made deaconess at 30, which was unusually young (*Life of Olympias* 6; E. A. Clark 1979: 123). The law of 390 required that a deaconess must be 60 years old and must have children; she is to entrust her property to suitable persons, retaining only the income.

Let her not, under the cover of religion, use up any of the jewellery and furniture, the gold and silver and other distinctions of an

---

[3] For detailed studies of these remarkable women, see Yarbrough (1976); E. A. Clark (1979, 1983a, 1984, 1986); Harries (1984), especially on the property aspect; Drijvers (1987). Salzmann (1989) warns against overstating the role of women in the 'Christianization' of the Roman aristocracy.

illustrious house; she must assign all to her children or her kinsfolk or to whatever others she chooses, and she is not to write as her heir, when her life ends, any church, cleric or poor person. (CT 16. 2. 27)

The historian Sozomen (*History of the Church* 7. 16, PG 67. 1461) says this law was prompted by a scandal in the Church at Constantinople: a lady of good family, who had been in church engaged in private penance, claimed that she had been raped (or seduced) by a deacon. If he is right, what we see here is not only a financial worry, but the long-standing belief that religion makes women vulnerable, because men from outside their families have access to their bodies and their property. This was the overt reason for Jerome's being asked to leave Rome (*Letter* 45, PL 22. 480–4); the anxiety reappears in a law of Justinian (*Nov.* J. 117. 15. 1, AD 542), which makes provision for the man who finds his wife or daughter conversing with someone in a holy place, and suspects their motives. It is also important that the men concerned were usually of much lower social status than the women—like Jerome in relation to Marcella and Paula, or John Chrysostom in relation to Olympias (E. A. Clark 1979: 60–70). From the aristocratic point of view, the legacy-hunter was at work again; from the clergy point of view (Brown 1987: 279) dependence on rich women was embarrassing.

Two months after the law was passed, the ban on leaving money to clergy was lifted (CT 16. 2. 28), but in tones which suggest ill-concealed fury. Disputes still arose. In 434 it was specified that the Church could inherit a deaconess's estate only (as with other clergy) if she died intestate and there were no other claimants (CT 5. 6. 3). Marcian (*Nov.* Marc. 5. 1, AD 455) examined the disputed will of one Hypatia, who had included the priest Anatolius among her heirs; he concluded that she had not neglected any who deserved well of her, and confirmed the right of a woman who has entered the religious life to leave property to the Church. But deaconesses, like other women, were subject to the double standard. A deacon who married, or took a concubine, was laicized; a deaconess (*Nov.* J. 6) was threatened with death.

A splendidly phrased law of 458 (*Nov.* Leo and Maj. 6)

covers several other problems. It declares that a girl committed to virginity by her parents cannot be consecrated and veiled until she is 40 (probably the age at which she is deemed to be past child-bearing: see below, Sect. 3.6). If she becomes legally independent (that is, if her father dies and she is of age) before 40, she may express a wish to marry and shall have her due inheritance. Childless widows who refuse to remarry are deemed to have a frivolous wish for freedom and attention: if under 40 and capable of bearing children, they must either remarry or divide their property with their kin. A widow with children need not remarry. Finally, the nuptial donation should be equivalent to the dowry, but there must be a dowry, and the donation cannot be extorted before the marriage takes place. (Had someone been arguing that marriage was a bad bet anyway?) It is the emperors' express hope that these measures will safeguard good relations between parents and children, child-bearing by women of good family, and religious observance freely chosen. Not surprisingly, many scholars have suspected (Drijvers 1987: 251) that, at least in the élite society which came to the emperor's notice, there was a shortage of suitable wives with dowries; and there is enough information to confirm that, in some of the greatest senatorial families, more family members remained unmarried in the fourth century than in earlier centuries (Corbier 1990).

2.8. *Women's Weakness*

Much of the legislation surveyed in these two chapters was inspired by a belief that women are weak, and need to be protected against exploitation and from the dangers of their own nature. What was this weakness? Women, it was thought, were physically hampered by lack of strength and especially by child-bearing. They were also under-educated and lacked experience of life; they were dependent, both for property and for advice, on their male relatives rather than on colleagues and contacts; they were emotionally vulnerable (Beaucamp 1990: 11–16).

Weakness was not consistently invoked, either in ideology or in law. For instance, it seems not to have dispensed women of low social status from condemnation to the mines (if only as camp-followers of the miners) or the imperial woollen mills (Millar 1984: 139, 145), from the more appalling physical penalties of late Roman law, or from the possibility of torture as part of a judicial enquiry—though pregnancy at least postponed this fate (D. 48. 19. 3). It is always a moot point whether these penalties were actually inflicted or were even meant to be inflicted (MacMullen 1986*b*, Brown 1981: ch. 6). But Jerome (*Letter* 1, PL 22. 326–31) describes a case at Vercelli, in his own time, in which a woman suspected of adultery was tortured to exact a confession when her supposed lover said he was innocent, and was sentenced to execution—which failed to kill her, since she was indeed innocent and was divinely protected.

Jerome's story repeats some of the more sinister themes of Christian romance: torture and botched execution of the innocent. Christian women were inspired (Averil Cameron 1991: 115) by the imagined story of Thecla, companion of Paul, who endured the fire and the wild beasts in the arena; and women martyrs—Christians before Constantine, victims of rival sects thereafter—are described suffering extremes of torture, often sexual. We have to ask whether the readers of Prudentius' poems on Eulalia and Agnes (*Peristephanon* 3, 14; PL 60. 341–57, 580–90), or of the martyrdom of Febronia (Brock and Harvey 1987: 150–76), wanted only to be reassured that the human spirit strengthened by Christ can withstand agony and degradation. The erotic content of hagiography and martyrology is only just beginning to be acknowledged (Brock and Harvey 1987; Kazhdan 1990).

But in some respects, weakness could be an advantage. Minors were excused ignorance of the law, and so were women (D. 22. 6. 9 pr.)—within limits, because the law was unwilling to assist negligence, or to allow gain which resulted from ignorance (CT 3. 5. 3, AD 330). Women were dispensed from the civic duties which men so often tried to escape (CT 12. 1. 137. 1, AD 393), though they might inherit the financial obligations without the status. For instance, if a man dies after his nomination as praetor, and leaves only daughters, they inherit his obligations, but 'it appears unlawful and disgraceful' for them to be given senatorial insignia (CT 6. 4. 17, AD 370). Women also, in some circumstances, had special legal protection. Justinian explained why he had changed his own earlier law on the right to reclaim dowry:

[the previous law] did not take into account the weakness [*fragilitas*] of women, nor that the husband enjoys their body, substance, and entire life, and for women almost all their substance consists in the dowry . . . Who does not pity them for their services to their husbands, the danger of childbirth, and indeed the bringing into life of children, on account of which our laws have introduced many privileges? (CJ 8. 17(18). 12, AD 531)

Similarly, he modified the second-century ruling that a mother could inherit from a child who died intestate only if she had borne three (or, if a freedwoman, four) children, and was not displaced by other heirs who took priority. The 'right of three children', which conferred various legal privileges, had been formulated (in the late first century BC) in order to encourage the propertied classes to reproduce; it could be acquired by a grant from the emperor. Justinian took a different line. 'We decided that the mother should be helped, having regard to nature and child-bearing and the danger and often death it brings to mothers . . . in what has she done wrong, if she has given birth not to many but to few?' (J. *Inst.* 3. 3. 4). The same protectiveness inspired his ruling (*Nov.* J. 134. 9, AD 556) that women were not to be imprisoned on ordinary charges such as debt: instead, sureties were to be found. (A law of 320 (CT 9. 3. 1), which attempts to mitigate the normal conditions of chaining and unhealthy confinement, shows what prison could be like even for those on remand.) If it was absolutely necessary to hold a woman, on a major criminal charge, she must be sent to a convent or guarded by reliable women, but not by men—who would, though he does not say so, probably abuse her, and certainly ruin her reputation.

Justinian's insistence on proper treatment for women has been illustrated several times in these chapters, and stands out in late Roman legislation (Jolowicz and Nicholas 1972: 507; Beaucamp 1990: 210); but it is not the whole story. From one point of view, weakness required protection; from another, it amounted to incompetence. 'Women's weakness' can imply disparagement or sympathy (Beaucamp 1976; Dixon 1984). Some ancient and modern opinion (Y. Thomas 1991) concluded that weakness was only an outmoded fiction, an attempt to establish and justify social patterns of power and inheritance. But, either way, women could not be expected to take on the responsibility for others which was characteristic of men.

One important consequence was that a woman could not act as guardian to her own children if her husband died. This question did not arise in classical Roman law, because a woman did not have *potestas*, legal control, over anyone. For the same reason, she could not adopt a child. Greek law had become more flexible, and Roman law had to take this into account. We find Diocletian making a concession to a woman living in Egypt who has lost her own sons and wants to adopt her son-in-law (CJ 8. 47(48). 5, AD 291). She cannot, strictly speaking, adopt, but she is allowed to establish a legal relationship, and the principle is generalized in later Roman law for women who have lost their children (J. *Inst.* 1. 11. 10). It had also become possible, in Greek tradition, for women to be guardians of their children, and some conflicts and ways round the law developed when Roman law prevailed after 212 (Modrzejewski 1970: 361). In Roman practice (Y. Thomas 1991: 126), as distinct from law, widows had been left in charge from the late second century, and ingenious legal devices had ensured that they were in control of the property which the children would inherit; whereas widows and divorcees had been bringing up children, with the nominal control of a guardian, at least since Cornelia mother of the Gracchi.

Diocletian made no concessions here. 'It is accepted that taking on the protection of another person is a man's job and beyond the female sex. So, if your son is under age, ask for a guardian for him' (rescript of Diocletian to Dionysia, CJ 2. 12. 18, AD 295). This was a reasonable position, because women were likely to be inexperienced and could be widowed very young, but it was modified because of another belief about women: they love their children. A mother could, as a rule, be trusted to act in her child's interest, as another guardian might not.

A law of 373 (CJ 5. 35. 2–3) gives preference to the guardian appointed by will, but, failing him, allows the mother or grandmother to be guardian—provided she swears not to remarry. (Given the age at which many women married, a grandmother might be in her late twenties.) No other woman was eligible (*Nov.* J. 118. 5 AD 543), and the female guardian was allowed to change her mind and hand over to a man. As we have seen (see above, Sect. 1.3), the underlying anxiety was that she might, if she remarried, divert her ward's inheritance to her second husband and their children. Unfortunately, the oath not to remarry was not taken very seriously. A law of 539 (*Nov.* J. 94) brings together an interesting range of attitudes. A mother need not be excluded from guardianship, as anyone else would be, on the grounds that she is a debtor or creditor of her children, 'because, as a rule, natural love and devotion to children removes any suspicion'. But, since women have often perjured themselves and remarried, the oath is replaced by a renunciation of the advantages given to women by the *senatusconsultum Velleianum*, and, of course, the guardianship is lost if the mother (or grandmother) does remarry.

The *senatusconsultum Velleianum* was a measure of the mid-first century AD, probably linked to the decision of the emperor Claudius to abolish guardianship of women by their male kin. This decision allowed some women to stand surety for the debts of people outside their family of birth, even if their dowry was thereby put at risk. Under Augustus, there had been a decision not to enforce a creditor's claim against a woman who had taken responsibility for her husband's debt: it was a basic principle of Roman law that the property of husband and wife remained separate unless she actually passed into his family (a form of marriage which had become obsolete in the later empire). The consuls now asked the senate to advise on obligations undertaken by women on behalf of others, and were assured (D. 16. 1. 2) that 'it is not equitable for women to undertake the duties of men, and be bound by any such obligations'. This principle also had the desired effect of safeguarding the woman's share of her family's property.

In practice, a woman's surety was accepted if it was clear that she had experience of financial matters and was not acting under constraint (Crook 1986). Justinian (CJ 4. 29. 22, AD 530) ruled that, provided she formally confirmed her intention, a woman could stand surety for anyone except her husband. But some women were genuinely in need of legal protection. Young widows, in particular, might have a very difficult time fending off the claims of relatives and making slaves obey instructions, as John Chrysostom's mother—widowed at twenty with two young children—told him (*On the Priesthood* 1. 5, PG 48. 624). This was the standard argument advanced by widows who wanted to remarry; sixth-century legal papyri (Beaucamp 1985) likewise show that widowhood was an independent but endangered state. Older widows might be inexperienced or impoverished; a poor widow was a typical object of charity, and only the Church, which discouraged her remarriage, would give her support and status. (In the early centuries there was an 'order of widows' committed to a life of prayer, but this pattern seems to have ended by the fourth century: instead, widows might join a community or serve as deaconesses, or at least be on the bishop's welfare list.) John Chrysostom emphasises bereaved and frightened women among those supported by the church at Antioch (*Homily on 1 Corinthians* 22, PG 57. 179), and points out to men who say they want to protect a helpless woman (*Against those men who cohabit with virgins* 7, PG 47. 594) that the city is full of maimed and destitute women—they do not have to select a pretty girl.

Some widows, on the other hand, were perfectly competent. It might not be proper for a woman to go out and make a profit, but her traditional role as guardian of the household property could supply plenty of financial experience (John Chrysostom, *Against Remarriage* 4, PG 48. 615). We may be suspicious when Sidonius (*Letter* 6. 2) pulls strings for a 'poor unprotected widow' whose daughter-in-law, having lost husband and son, would prefer to stay with her—there is a lot of money at stake. And it would have been absurd to invoke the *senatusconsultum Velleianum* in favour of (for example) Emmelia, mother of Basil and of Gregory of Nyssa, who was widowed after the birth of nine children, paid taxes in three provinces, and saw four sons and four daughters creditably established in the State, the Church, or marriage before joining her daughter Macrina in home-based asceticism; or in favour of Amanda, wife of Aper, who took over the management of the family property so as to free him to lead the ascetic life (Paulinus, *Letter* 44. 4, PL 61. 388). So, in effect, the law of 539 says that the woman cannot have her cake and eat it: if she really wants to take on the manly task of being a guardian, legally responsible for a child, she cannot claim to be a weak woman in need of legal protection. The law, as the emperor Alexander Severus tartly remarked (CJ 4. 29. 5, AD 224), is supposed to benefit women's weakness, not their ingenuity in law-evasion.

3

HEALTH

MEDICINE was part of the lives of ordinary women. They were agents as well as patients, the first line of defence against illness. Hospitals were available, as one form of Christian charity, from the late fourth century, but sick people who had homes were usually nursed there: women supervised diet and tried out traditional remedies. Some women were acknowledged experts on illness and medicines generally; others specialized in childbirth and the problems associated with reproductive life, including 'female complaints' and sexual difficulties. It was easier and cheaper to call on them than to employ a doctor with a professional training.

Much of what was said above about our information on late Roman law applies also to late Roman medicine. Medicine, like law, is known more from textbooks than from reports of practice. When we do hear about doctors in action, it is often from hagiographies, which emphasize the huge fees doctors charge, their painful remedies, and their failure to cure the patient, in contrast to the immediate healing performed by the saint (examples in Patlagean 1977: 103–4). The problems of using medical texts for information about women are similar to those of using legal texts. Until the 1970s there was a feeling that medicine—like law—reached its peak in the second century, with Galen, and that later texts repeat the discoveries of the past rather than making new ones. Some texts survive in later extracts and transcripts, though these are more extensive than for law; gynaecology is only a small proportion of the total material; and there is not nearly as much help available on late antique medical texts as there is on the works which supplied most of their subject-matter, namely the Hippocratic Corpus and the writings of Galen himself.[1]

There is also, as for law, the problem of how the surviving texts relate to society, because so much material is reused and newly presented. Some disagreements among doctors are reported, but much information is repeated from century to century and we do not know enough about new discoveries or local differences of technique or belief. In particular, the *Gynaecology* of Soranus, a handbook for intelligent midwives written in the second century, was translated (from Greek into Latin) or paraphrased in many later texts, and modern writers are tempted to use it as a timeless guide to pregnancy, childbirth, baby care, and female medical problems throughout the ancient world. (It was still in use as a textbook in the eighteenth century.)

Finally, the authors of the medical texts were usually men with a formal medical training, and they were often at the top of their profession. Galen was court physician to Marcus Aurelius and Commodus in the late second century, Oribasius to Julian in the mid-fourth century, Aetius of Amida to Justinian in the early sixth century. So we may suspect the usual class bias: their female patients were (probably) rich enough to hire them rather than other kinds of healer. They may have had more extensive experience as doctors employed by a city, though none is known to have done so. City doctors were under at least moral pressure (Nutton 1977: 211) to treat the poor, but it was, apparently, worth a mention when they actually did. Jacobus Psychrestos (so called for his favourite 'cooling' technique), an *archiatros* of Constantinople, treated the poor free of charge; others, to judge from popular wariness of doctors (Horden 1982), were beyond the means of the poor.

If the class bias is not certain, the male voice is; but it may sometimes be reporting what women said. One major difference between law and medicine is that medicine concerned with women was shaped not only by the questions and

---

[1] So far, only Soranus is easily available in well-annotated translations: see Short References, and Jackson (1988, 1990) for further bibliography. Hopkins (1965a: 133–4) tabulates medical writers concerned with contraception. See further Duffy (1984), Nutton (1984), Vikan (1984), all from a *Symposium on Byzantine Medicine*; Temkin (1991) for Hippocratic medicine.

complaints of women, but by their analysis of what was wrong and their experience of how to treat it. Doctors were heavily dependent on information given by female patients and by midwives, and may not always have been able to confirm it by observation. Some doctors were aware of the results of dissection: for instance, Soranus and Galen knew that the uterus does not in fact become displaced and wander round the body (see below, Sect. 3.2). But it appears that human dissection was no longer practised in later antiquity, and that only the Alexandria medical school studied anatomy on the human skeleton (Edelstein 1967). There were other possibilities: medical equipment included the vaginal speculum (illustrated in Jackson 1990: 9), and some patients allowed doctors to conduct internal or external examinations.

Some, but not all. Gregory of Nazianzus reports that his sister Gorgonia refused examination by male doctors after a serious accident (*In Praise of his sister Gorgonia* 15, PG 35. 808), and Gregory of Nyssa says that his sister Macrina healed by prayer a breast abcess which she refused to show to a doctor (*Life of Macrina* 31, PG 46. 992). Each brother mentions his sister's refusal as worthy of praise. These may be exceptional cases; but there are other indications that standards of modesty changed. Late-antique clothes, on the evidence of art, revealed far less of the body than had previously been acceptable. A fourth-century treatise on virginity informs its female readers that nudity, even in front of another woman, is unacceptable except in great need, and that a consecrated virgin should not even look at her own naked body (PG 28. 264). Late-antique housing may show an increased concern for privacy in baths and latrines. Christian women were urged to avoid the public baths if they could, and it was a sign of virtue that Olympias never bathed naked. Perhaps, then, medical examination became more of an ordeal. In the Hippocratic tradition, 'fear, shame and inexperience' might prevent a woman patient from confiding in a doctor, though time and necessity usually brought her to it in the end. Doctors accepted what they were told by women whom they judged to be experienced, and who could carry out self-examination and treatment, but insisted on examining those whom they thought unreliable reporters

(King 1985: 148; Hanson 1990: 309). We simply do not know how much women told their doctors, how well the doctors understood it, or how much they were allowed to see.

3.1. Medical Skills

People calling themselves *medici* were an odd mixture of the very highly selected and the self-appointed, with a wide range of ability, qualifications, and prestige. (George Eliot describes a comparable situation, in provincial England about 1830, in *Middlemarch*.) Some efforts were made to impose order and hierarchy, particularly among the court doctors (Nutton 1977). Top-level doctors were trained at the medical schools of the great cities, by lectures, demonstrations, and practice. There is a question about the proportion of practice to theory in their training. In the University of Constantinople, established by Theodosius II in 425, medical lectures were part of the philosophy course (Vogel 1967); this is reasonable, since philosophy, in the ancient world, included the natural sciences and mathematics. Surviving lecture notes from Alexandria (Duffy 1984), most famous of all the medical schools, show that the course there expounded selected works from the Hippocratic Corpus (mostly from the fourth and fifth centuries BC) and the extensive writings of Galen, who had himself complained that medical lectures were too theoretical.

Hippocratic medicine had been concerned to establish itself as a *technê*, a skill founded on an impressive structure of theory (King 1985: 61), as opposed to simple experience of remedies and therapies which healers (often women healers) had found to work. The balance between theory and practice may have shifted: in late antiquity it was high, but not automatic, praise of a doctor to say that he combined theory with experience. Eunapius (*Lives* 499), praising the doctor Ionicus, says that his skills included bandaging, amputation, and the use of drugs—and other doctors said that he made them understand material in older medical texts which had previously meant nothing to them. But we do have evidence for young men 'doing the rounds' with experienced doctors, and for apprenticeships, or owners training slaves, lower down the social scale. It is not clear (Miller 1985; Nutton 1986) that hospitals became centres of care and training.

Some women described themselves, or were described by others, as *medica* (Longfield Jones 1986: 81; Jackson 1988: 86–7). These women could not attend university lectures or train with doctors, but midwives and nursing attendants could work with doctors, and women caring for the sick could listen as the doctor explained the case to his trainees. According to Soranus (*Gyn.* 1. 1. 3) the 'complete midwife' understood all the branches of medicine: dietetics, pharmacy, and *cheirourgia*—that is the 'manual work' which includes massage and manipulation as well as the use of instruments. It is not clear that women ever performed surgery: a midwife had to be able to cut the umbilical cord safely, but so far as the evidence goes it was the doctor who was called in to perform embryotomy, the dissection *in utero* of a foetus which could not be delivered intact. Soranus wrote explicitly for midwives, whose clients would be impressed by knowledge of the female body, but women could also use other medical textbooks. Some surviving texts look very expensive, but there were shorter 'medical catechisms' (including one by Caelius Aurelianus), and working texts could be passed around and annotated. One fourth-century example (Youtie 1985) survives on papyrus.

There is at least a case for saying that medical writing, from the third century on, grows less concerned with general theory and more concerned with the material in earlier texts which is of practical use (Nutton 1984: 3–4). Oribasius and others compiled material on the assumption that educated persons can understand medicine: unfortunately for us, they appear far more interested in the everyday health of men than in that of women (Rousselle 1988: ch. 2). Marcellus of Bordeaux (Matthews 1971; Brown 1981: 113–17), who had been a high-ranking official of Theodosius I, wrote his *On Remedies* to enable his readers to be cured without resorting to doctors; he refers to three other praetorian prefects who had medical knowledge. They may have found it very necessary when they were away from the major cities—or even when they were not. Sidonius (*Letter* 2. 12) thinks his ailing daughter, who has a persistent cough accompanied by fever, will do better out of town and away from the advice of doctors, 'who sit by the bed and disagree, and who with their lack of learning and excess of zeal most dutifully kill many patients'.

Medical texts also include traditional remedies, the *pharmakeia* ranging from herbal medicine to white magic which had been especially, though not exclusively, women's area of expertise. These texts, once treated with contempt,[2] are now being surveyed for usable remedies (Riddle 1985, 1991). Marcellus sought information even from uneducated country people. He includes both incantations and 'polypharmacy', remedies with multiple ingredients which sound impressive but are likely to diminish the overall effect. As for amulets, many doctors endorsed the opinion of Soranus: 'the use of these things should not be prevented, for, even if they have no direct effect, they may improve the patient's morale through hope' (*Gyn.* 3. 10. 42).

So women could have learnt medicine from textbooks, practice, and association with experts, whether professionally trained male doctors or experienced women healers. We are reduced to guesswork and anecdote for how they actually did learn. Ausonius, writing in late-fourth-century Gaul, describes Aemilia, an early example of the maiden aunt (*Parentalia* 1. 6), who disliked being female and chose virginity. She also had a masculine pet-name, Hilarus, because from babyhood she looked like a cheerful (*hilarus*) boy; she 'practised the arts of medicine in the way men do', which may suggest a full-time commitment. Ausonius' father, her brother-in-law, was also a doctor who treated the poor free of charge (*Parentalia* 1. 13–14, *Epicedion* 11–12).

The Roman aristocrat Fabiola, praised by Jerome (*Letter* 77. 6, PL 22. 694), showed her Christian devotion by founding a hospital and nursing in it. We do not know what level of medical skill was offered, by her or anyone else, in this place of refuge for the destitute sick: Jerome is interested in her readiness to give nursing care to the most revolting illnesses. When Flacilla, wife of Theodosius I, helped in the hospitals of Constantinople (also in the late fourth century), it was remarkable

---

[2] 'Even the herbal works of Dioskurides, Galen and Oribasius were too difficult for the wilting mind of the Dark Ages' (Singer 1927: 31).

enough that she brought the patients their soup and bread and medicine, helped to feed them, and washed the bowl afterwards (Theodoret, *History of the Church* 5. 18. 2–3, PG 82. 1238). Nikarete, a self-effacing nun, prepared medicines for the poor, and often (according to Sozomen, *History of the Church* 8. 23, PG 67. 1576) did her relatives more good than the doctors could. The most splendid herbal to survive from late antiquity, the Vienna Dioscorides, was written for presentation to Anicia Juliana, daughter of an emperor and patron of the great church of S. Polyeuktos in Constantinople (Harrison 1989), around 512—but this is no proof that she read it. She certainly did not carry it around for consultation: it weighs fourteen pounds.[3]

A midwife was likely to be called in only for women patients, but her skill was not restricted to labour and delivery. Many illnesses in women were ascribed to problems with the uterus or to the retention of menstrual or lochial blood. John Chrysostom describes a virgin falling ill, the maidservants reluctantly getting up, someone going for the midwife, other young women coming round to help—and in the midst an unembarrassed male cohabitant (*That women under rule should not cohabit with men* 8, PG 47. 528). Jerome, cruder as usual, tells an ascetic young woman in Gaul of the servants' gossip about the young monk who lives with her and her mother. 'They say he sits by the bed, calls the midwives [*obstetrices*] when you are unwell, brings the chamber-pot, warms the linen cloths, folds the bandages' (*Letter* 117. 8, PL 22. 958).[4]

Midwifery was not necessarily a full-time job: Eunapius (*Lives* 463) happens to mention a skilled midwife who was also the hostess in one of the more exclusive Roman wine-bars, and was called to an emergency delivery while she was mixing a drink. But we hear also of women who carry on a surreptitious trade in charms and potions which are not dignified as medicines, and whose ignorance or malice may harm the patient or damage a new baby. Eusebia, wife of Constantius II, allegedly died from the treatment given her by a woman who

---

[3] I owe this information to Vivian Nutton, who points out that many herbals were obviously for admiration rather than for practical use, and hence survive in remarkably good condition.

[4] Are these perhaps menstrual cloths? See Sect. 3.4.

said she could restore the uterus; and Eusebia, allegedly, had herself made Helena, wife of the emperor Julian, take a drug which made her miscarry in every pregnancy (Holum 1982: 28).

3.2. The Female Human

It is not only medical texts which offer accounts of the human body. Theologians also describe the wonderful works of God, and, though their purpose is different from that of medical writers, they may share an educated interest in medicine (D. S. Wallace-Hadrill 1968: 59–60). The Judaeo-Christian creation story describes how God made woman from Adam's rib, bone of his bone and flesh of his flesh. But how much, in philosophical and medical theory, does a woman resemble a man? Is she (Sissa 1991) a quite different kind of creature, or a variation on the norm?

Soranus (*Gyn.* 2. 57) reports medical disagreement on this point from the fourth-century BC on. Some doctors argued that there are diseases peculiar to women; others, like Soranus himself, that women experience conditions (such as pregnancy and lactation) which are peculiar to them, but that their diseases have the same basic causes as those of men and can be treated in the same way. Again, some doctors held that a woman, to be in good health, must make use of her reproductive system, whereas Soranus believed that a healthy life is possible (or more likely) for a woman whose body is not disrupted by intercourse or menstruation.

Hippocratic medical writing (King 1985: 119–48; Hanson 1990: 317–18) postulates that female flesh differs from male flesh: it is spongier and absorbs more blood from the digestive process. Women, being (mostly) sedentary, do not use up the surplus blood in strenuous exercise; women who do exercise, like singers and gymnasts, find that menstruation stops (a finding confirmed in present-day athletes). If the body is using the surplus for the growth of an embryo, or transforming it into milk, the blood does not need to be shed in menstruation. This theory explained why women do not menstruate in pregnancy (or at most experience slight cyclical bleeding), and also gave a reason for abstaining from sex during lactation, for fear a new pregnancy would divert the surplus needed for milk. But it followed that, in a woman not pregnant or lactating, the surplus had to be disposed of somehow. Absence or delay of menstruation was thus a serious concern, and many medical problems in women were ascribed to retention of blood. The other major cause of trouble was held to be a displaced uterus. It was believed that a uterus which became too dry—usually from lack of intercourse—moved in search of moisture; it might tip, so that menstrual blood could no longer be shed through the cervix, or, worse, it might attach itself to other organs of the body, exerting pressure or causing obstructions. 'Uterine suffocation' (Riddle 1985: 35) was held to produce a range of alarming symptoms. Hippocratic doctors argued that, since these experiences were peculiar to women, it made no sense to treat a woman patient in the same way as a man patient, for, even if their symptoms appeared to be the same, the cause might be quite different (Dean-Jones 1989; Hanson 1990).

By contrast, late-antique medical texts, like those of the first and second centuries (King 1985: 125), tend to emphasize the similarity of male and female, or to imply it by focusing on the male and rarely noting any divergence (Hanson 1990: 330–4; Laqueur 1990: ch. 2). General medical texts note a difference of treatment only where there is an obvious physical difference —as in the case of urinary ailments. Dissection had revealed that the uterus is secured by ligaments and cannot move around; absence of menstruation still caused concern, but was more likely to be taken as a symptom than as a cause. The underlying cause of disease, according to Soranus, is excessive constriction or relaxation; according to Galen, it is an imbalance in hot and cold, wet and dry. This applies to either sex, with due regard to the condition and environment of the individual patient. Treatises on 'women's concerns' (*gynaikeia*) apply the same basic medical principles to the female reproductive system. And even the reproductive system was held to have the same basic structure in male and female.

Nemesius of Emesa, a fourth-century writer with medical

and philosophical interests (probably just the kind of educated reader whom Marcellus of Bordeaux had in mind), offers a detailed physical description of humans. Only the section on reproduction is differentiated between male and female; and there, having described the male reproductive system, he observes (quoting Galen) that 'women too have all the same parts as men, but inside and not outside' (*On the Nature of Man* 25, PG 40. 701). This may sound improbable, but it made sense. The ovaries, known since the investigations of Herophilus in the third century BC, were generally interpreted as internal testes: the question was whether they refined the surplus blood enough to produce female seed.[5] Some theorists held that the embryo was formed from male and female seed, and was nourished with the blood which would otherwise have been shed in menstruation. Following Galen, they interpreted the Fallopian tubes as sperm-ducts which led to the uterus at the top of the vagina. Others (including Soranus) held that menstrual blood was the only female contribution to the embryo. Following Herophilus, they argued that the Fallopian tubes led to the bladder, and that the female seed was simply excreted—which seems pointless.

Nemesius continues:

> Aristotle and Democritus want the woman's seed to contribute nothing to the procreation of children: they want the secretion of women to be a sweat from the part, rather than seed. But Galen, criticizing Aristotle, says women do produce seed and the mixture of both seeds makes the embryo: that is why intercourse is called *mixis* [mixing]. But the [woman's] seed is not as perfect as that of the man, but still unrefined and moist; and since it is like that, the [woman's] seed is nourishment for that of the man. (*On the Nature of Man* 25, PG 40. 701)

There was no doubt in late antiquity (as there had been in classical Athens) that the mother actually contributed to the formation of the child, rather than being as it were the earth in which the seed was sown. Stoics, who held that the soul is material (though a very refined and subtle matter), agreed that

---

[5] See further Waszink (1947: 342–5); Perrin (1981: ch. 5); Boylan (1984); Blayney (1986); Jacquart and Thomasset (1988: 61–70).

the mother contributed elements of soul as well as body (Waszink 1947: 342–5). But the female contribution was not thought to be equal to that of the male, and it seemed obvious that the male seed initiates the process of generation. This belief had an important effect (E. A. Clark 1986: 311) on Augustine's doctrine of original (sexually transmitted) sin. Augustine finds it surprising that Paul says 'sin entered the world through one man' (Rom. 5: 12) rather than through one woman, Eve. He suggests an explanation: it is the vitiated seed of the male, infected by the lust which is biologically necessary for the discharge of semen, which actually generates the child.

What determined the sex of the embryo? The important factors were taken to be the predominance of male over female seed, or vice versa; the location of the embryo in the womb; and the available warmth. Different combinations of factors resulted in girls who look like their fathers not their mothers, and so on. Galen's version was that females, being colder than males, produce thinner and weaker seed; and also that female-ness is associated with the colder seed which is delivered via the left-hand seminal duct in either sex, maleness with the warmer seed which is delivered via the right-hand duct. The left-hand side of the uterus is thus colder, and that is where girl babies grow.

Relative lack of warmth was a useful all-purpose explanation of femaleness, which allowed for the basic similarity of males and females. In both sexes, the surplus which is not needed for maintenance is available for reproduction, but in males it is refined as semen, in females it (or most of it) remains as blood. The female reproductive organs remain inside the body because there is not enough heat to push them outside. Lack of vital heat could also account for other supposedly female charac-teristics, notably physical and intellectual inferiority. But it does not imply that the female is a different kind of human: she is an only slightly modified male.

3.3. *Virginity*

Late-antique beliefs about virginity appear to be more precise than in earlier Greek culture (Sissa 1990): they focus on the 'integrity' of the woman, and this seems to mean an unbroken hymen. Soranus (*Gyn.* 1. 5, followed by Oribasius *Medical Collections* 24. 37) says firmly that neither examination nor dissection confirms the belief that a thin membrane seals the vagina and is broken by defloration, or by menstruation if that comes first. This belief suggests that pre-pubertal defloration was a least a recognized possibility: it has sometimes (Rousselle 1991: 328–9) been thought necessary so that the first menstruation can escape. Soranus holds that, if a membrane which closes the vagina is found, it is the pathological condition *atrêsia*. Current opinion is that, if he refers to a hymen, he overstates the case: there is one, but it usually perforates long before puberty, and physical exercise encourages this.

But midwives who had not read their Soranus went on doing tests for virginity. Their results conflicted (according to Ambrose: *Letter* 5b, PL 16. 891), but educated men still believed the tests to be conclusive. A law of Constantine (CT 9. 8, ?AD 326, Interpretation) was taken to imply that, when a guardian has been living with his female ward, she must be proved to be a virgin before she marries. John Chrysostom claims that midwives were always running to the houses of virgin cohabitants who took, or refused, tests to demonstrate their continued virginity (*That women under rule should not cohabit with men* 2, PG 47. 516)—just as people have their slaves tested on purchase. Augustine (*City of God* 1. 18, PL 41. 31–2) reports that a clumsy midwife herself destroyed the integrity she was supposed to investigate—not, he adds, that this has any significance for the woman's vow of chastity, any more than the rape of consecrated virgins by Goths at the sack of Rome. When he imagines (*City of God* 14. 26, PL 41. 434) what pro-creation would have been like if the human race had not fallen into sin, he suggests:

It would have been possible then for the male seed to be discharged into the uterus of the wife, the integrity of the female genitalia being preserved, just as it is now possible for the flow of menstrual blood to be discharged from the uterus of a virgin, that same integrity being preserved.

Perhaps he had absorbed one of Soranus's anti-hymen arguments, namely that a hymen which closed the vagina would prevent menstruation, but still thought there was some physical sign of virginity.

Such beliefs are manifested in the popular story of Salome the midwife (*Protevangelium of James* 19–20), who refused to accept, until she did the test, the virginity of Mary after the birth of Jesus. (The hand with which she investigated shrivelled, until the new-born healed it.) In the late fourth century there was theological controversy about *virginitas in partu*, that is, the doctrine that the birth of Jesus made no change to the physical virginity of Mary. Jovinian was able to argue that *virgo concepit, non virgo generavit*—'she conceived as a virgin, she did not give birth as a virgin'—because he and his readers (cf. E. A. Clark 1986: 406–7) were thinking in terms of the physical impact of giving birth; perhaps even in terms of post-partum changes, noted by Soranus, in the size of the uterus and the state of the cervix. Jovinian's immediate purpose (Hunter 1987) was to argue that virginity is not superior to marriage and child-bearing as a Christian way of life; there is a further question about incarnation, which for him and for many others requires the real physical birth of the real human being Jesus.

Jovinian was in the minority, at least among fourth-century Christians, as regards the value of marriage. There was some resistance (Hunter 1987, 1989) to ascetic disparagement of marriage and child-bearing, and Christian writers are not prepared to denounce marriage and procreation: to do so would go against Scripture and would imply that the world God made is not worth continuing. But they do advocate both male and female virginity, often by emphasizing the seamy side of marriage and child-bearing, and the pain, illness, and anxiety that virgin women will escape. Some writers on virginity were impressed by those who chose celibacy in widowhood, knowing what they were missing, but the preference was for those who remained virgin all their lives. Virginity is presented as a return to the natural human condition, the life of Paradise before Eve and Adam disobeyed God. There was an interesting debate (E. A. Clark 1986: 353–85) on whether Adam and Eve were in fact virgin in Paradise, or whether they had a sex-life free from uncontrollable lust and from pain. Either way, it was Eve's punishment to bring forth children in pain and to feel desire for her husband, who would be her master: virgins could escape this penalty.

Non-Christians were likely to agree that sexual desire was potentially disruptive and dangerous, and that its only legitimate use was for the procreation of children within marriage. But in the general view (shared by many Christians: E. A. Clark 1983b; Pagels 1988), sexual desire was part of human nature, provided to ensure the continuance of the human race. There was no encouragement for non-Christian women to choose virginity (see, further, below, Sect. 5.3). Soranus (*Gyn.* 1. 7. 32) was able to find some examples of women, presumably not Christian, who were celibate by law and in the service of the god, and argued that women were the healthier for not experiencing the disruptions of intercourse and pregnancy: they had menstrual problems only if they put on weight and took no exercise. (Unfortunately, there are no medical reports on the Vestal Virgins, who would have made a most interesting sample.) But these cults were exceptional in Graeco-Roman religion, and Soranus was in opposition to the most-used medical writings. The Hippocratic texts (cf. Hanson 1989: 302–4) tend to regard pregnancy, or at least intercourse, as essential to female health and a cure for much female illness: by these means the uterus is kept moist and in place, and the surplus blood is either used or enabled to be shed. Galen thought that celibacy in either sex was actually a health risk, causing problems from the retention of (male or female) seed.[6]

3.4. Puberty and Desire

Medical writers expected menarche in the fourteenth year (Amundsen and Diers 1969). We do not know whether this refers to the first signs of menstruation or to the establishment of regular periods; or indeed whether the figure derives from observation rather than from a belief in seven-year phases of life. 'After twice seven years, [the human being] reaches

[6] Late-antique attitudes to virginity and sexuality have been exhaustively discussed, especially by Brown (1988), who gives a full bibliography. His ch. 17 is especially relevant here. See also Averil Cameron (1989, 1991).

1. Marriage-ring showing Christ and Mary between the couple: the word is *(h)omonoia*, "concord".

2. Amulet ring: the many-rayed figure is a *chnoubis*, used to invoke calm for the intestines or the uterus. Inscribed "Lord, help the wearer [feminine]".

3. Ivory relief showing the Magi bringing offerings to Christ. Lower panel: the midwife Salome shows her withered hand to the newborn Christ for healing.

4. Ivory diptych showing Asclepius (son of the healing god Apollo) and Hygeia, the personification of Health. The child to the left of Asclepius wears a hooded *cilicium*.

5. Mosaic from San Vitale, Ravenna (dedicated 547) showing the empress Theodora and her court ladies taking

puberty by necessity of age: the force of generation begins in males, purgation in females' (Macrobius, *On the Dream of Scipio* 1. 6. 71). It was recognized that diet and life-style made a difference to the surplus available for menstruation, and potentially for pregnancy, so menarche could be delayed by exercise (ball-games and singing in girls' choruses) or encouraged by extra food and rest. Soranus reports (*Gyn.* 1. 6. 27) that some people thought menstruation was good for women, because it disposed of their surplus: he thought it was disruptive, just as intercourse and pregnancy are, and points to the example of healthy non-menstruating women. He did overestimate normal blood loss.

Quite how women coped with menstruation is, as usual, unknown. Soranus says (*Gyn.* 1. 5. 26) that grown women know what discharge is normal for them, and what their needs are for rest or activity: there is wide variation, and one should leave it to them. Sanitary protection, to use the modern euphemism, consisted of cloths and, at a guess, wool (soft, absorbent, and in general medical use for pessaries); we do not know how they were kept in place. (Something may be learnt from the methods and materials used in the early twentieth century, before disposable towels were available and cheap: Bullough 1985.) They were called, in Greek, *phulakia* (protection again), and we hear about them in an unexpected context.

The Souda (an encyclopaedia compiled in the tenth century) tells the story of Hypatia and her choice not to marry. One of her students fell in love with her, and she discouraged him by throwing a used menstrual cloth in his face. That, she said, was what he loved, not anything beautiful: by which she meant (Schanzer 1985) that, instead of directing his desire to the unchanging truths, which alone are beautiful, he was allowing himself to be distracted by physical desires and the messy business of continuing this impermanent world. It had a powerful effect on him. The Souda also informs us that the holy philosopher Heraiskos (on whom see Bowersock 1990: 60) was so sensitive to this contrast that he got a headache if he heard a menstruating woman speak—he could tell; and that there were in Alexandria women called *kērukainai*, who went to houses and apartments to collect used *phulakia*, which they threw into the sea (salt water was a traditional purifier). All these fascinating items may be derived from the *Life of Isidore the Philosopher* by Damascius (frs. *102-4 Zintzen).

If this was the philosophical approach to menstruation, it was not likely to encourage the positive attitude which educated women are supposed to have today. Porphyry (*On Abstinence* 2. 50) lists menstruating women, along with tombs, sacrilegious men, sexual intercourse, and disturbing sights and sounds, as something avoided by priests and seers. This may owe more to high philosophical doctrine than to ordinary cult-rules (but see Parker 1983: 100-3). Christian tradition did not take over Jewish purity regulations, which aimed to safeguard men from cultic pollution acquired by contact with a menstruating woman (Wegner 1988: 18). But it did take over the story in which the messiness, pain, and desire inherent in the reproductive cycle are Eve's punishment for disobedience; and there was a fascinating medieval debate (Wood 1981) on whether Mary had to share the female experience of menstruation, or was exempt from it as from the pain of childbirth. So far as I know, 'the curse' (of Eve) does not yet appear as a nickname for menstruation, which in medical texts is usually called 'monthlies' (*katamēnia*), or 'purge' (*katharsis*) (see, further, King 1985: 243)—but we have no idea what ordinary women called it. The same problem arises in the seventeenth century (Crawford 1981), even though more writing by women is available; many medical texts were still using Hippocrates, Aristotle, and Galen.

Menstruation was widely associated with female desire, perhaps by assimilation to oestrus in other mammals, perhaps by observation either of sexual feeling or of the effects of fasting. Modern research suggests both that fasting reduces libido (Musurillo 1956) and that it is likely to produce amenorrhea if a woman's body weight drops below eight stone. Voluntary fasting was the standard technique for ascetic women who wished to fight desire, and the connection between fasting and amenorrhea may also have been known (Rousselle 1988: ch. 10), although the texts do not make it explicit.

Conversely, medical texts suggest that the best time for

conception is at the end of a period, when the uterus is not
overloaded and the desire is there. Soranus (*Gyn.* 1. 10. 37)
says there will not be conception without desire; in cases of
conception from rape, the desire was there but obscured by the
judgement. He does not suggest that female orgasm is necessary for conception (see, further, Laqueur 1990; E. A. Clark
1986: 299), or that desire will not occur at other times. Nemesius notes (*On the Nature of Man* 25, PG 40. 701) that female
humans, unlike other female animals, allow intercourse even
when they are already pregnant: he thinks this is because they
have free will, instead of being compelled by Nature.

Intercourse during menstruation (ranked with adultery in
Leviticus 18: 19) was said by Christian writers to produce de-
formed children (Noonan 1966: 85, Wood 1981: 716). Medical
texts say only that conception during menstruation is unlikely, since the uterus is engaged in disposing of surplus
rather than retaining it. Christian texts in fact say very little
about menstruation, which could remain private, though the
discomforts of pregnancy and the pains of childbirth are
lavishly described in the interests of virginity. Sometimes it
was necessary to discuss the question whether a menstruating
woman may approach the altar for communion; Jewish tradition certainly, and Greek tradition probably (Parker 1983:
100–3), would require her to stay clear of holy places when she
was polluted by bloodshed. Dionysius of Alexandria (*Canonical
Letter* 2, PG 10. 1281) thought there was no problem: surely no
woman would want to take communion in the circumstances?
The woman with a discharge of blood (Luke 8: 43–4) ventured
only to touch the hem of Jesus' cloak. A contemporary Syrian
text (Cohen 1991: 287–90) uses the same story to argue that a
menstruating woman may have contact with holy things.
Gregory the Great (*Letter* 11. 64, PL 77. 1196), answering a
question from Augustine of Canterbury, observed that menstruating women—and men who had had seminal emissions
—did usually abstain, not because they were contaminated but
because of the emotional turmoil which accompanied the physical event. But, he said, menstruation is natural, and he was
prepared only to commend women who abstained, not to

exclude those who did not. All human infirmity, not just this, is a result of the Fall. Unfortunately (Cohen 1991: 298–9), this sensible view did not prevail.

Menarche and marriage tended to go together. Doctors were well aware that pregnancy was dangerous until the girl had finished growing: menarche shows that the uterus is functioning, but childbirth could still be difficult (Soranus, *Gyn.* 1. 8. 33). It seems likely too that many menstrual problems referred to doctors were not problems at all, but the variable cycles which occur over two years or so until menstruation is fully established. But, on the assumption that menstruation and desire are linked, early marriage was one way of keeping young people out of moral danger or social disgrace. The minimum age for legally valid marriage was 12: 'women are always assumed to have reached puberty by their twelfth birthday' (CJ 5. 60. 3, AD 529). Some people evidently thought that appropriate. Gregory of Nyssa describes the twelfth year as that 'in which the flower of youth chiefly begins to shine out' (*Life of Macrina* 4, PG 46. 964): his sister Macrina was already betrothed. Similarly, Prudentius (*Peristephanon* 3. 12, 110; PL 60. 342, 348) describes the 12-year-old Eulalia as ready for marriage. Ausonius wrote an epitaph (*Epitaphs* 35) for the 16-year-old Anicia, who had led a full life: 'she married, she conceived, she gave birth' (and she died while still feeding her baby). But we simply do not have the data to show what was the preferred age of marriage, even with computer-simulations and UN population tables to help (Hopkins 1965b; Frier 1982; Shaw 1987).

There have been several attempts to deduce marriage-age, and other family patterns, from tombstones, but we have to allow for regional and other variations both in marriage-age and in the commemoration of the dead. For instance (Shaw 1984: 467–72), Christian tombstones, in the western empire, typically use space to record the virtues of the deceased, not his or her family relationships; senators, and also soldiers, appear to emphasize different points. There is also the practical question (Mann 1985) whether good stone is readily available. Urban and rural patterns may well be different. It has been suggested (Hopkins 1965b) that Christian girls typically married at 15–18 rather than 12–15, but there is no conclusive evidence that Christian practice on marriage-age differed from non-Christian (Shaw 1987). There was certainly regional variation in the age at which women were allowed to reject marriage and take vows of virginity, and this may reflect differences in the preferred age of marriage. In the late fourth century, Basil of Caesarea, in Asia Minor, advocated delay to 16 or 17; a North African council chose 20. By contrast, a Spanish council insisted on 40, and the emperor Leo (*Nov.* Leo and Maj. 6, AD 458) seems to have agreed that this was the age at which marriage was no longer in question (see below, Sect. 3.6).

3.5. Fertility

Pregnancy, its absence or its avoidance, was a constant concern of women of reproductive age. Infertility was a tragedy which drove women to seek help from elusive saints or from other divine powers. Theodoret was conceived by the prayers of Macedonius, when his mother—then aged 30—had long accepted her infertility (*History of the Monks of Syria* 13, PG 82. 1407): she had been married for thirteen years. The philosopher Theosebius, who married only for the sake of children, expelled a demon from his infertile wife (Damascius, fr. 56 Zintzen); Zachariah of Mitylene (*Life of Severus*, PO 2. 17–19) tells the story of a high official, married to a woman of distinguished family, who was conned into believing that Isis would grant him a child. Women also wore amulets—not approved by Caesarius (*Sermon* 51. 4)—which symbolized a womb lying quiet, or securely closed upon its developing embryo (Vikan 1984: 77–8, with illustrations).

Childbirth, of course, could kill. The suggestions of Oribasius (*To Eunapius* 4. 113) for dealing with difficult labours are a range of herbal potions, a bath with a herbal infusion, making the patient sneeze, and tying a jasper-stone or a dry cyclamen root to the thigh. Melania the Younger (*Life of Melania* 61), saved a woman whose baby had died during labour but could not be delivered, even by embryotomy: the woman 'could neither live nor die'. (Melania's method was a Christianization of the ancient belief that the child cannot be delivered while things on and around the mother are tied up—for instance, her belt and her hair. She unfastened her own belt, which had belonged to a saint, and gave it to the woman to hold.) Megetia, a lady of Carthage, was also unable to deliver a seven-month child who had died in the womb. She had dislocated her jaw by excessive vomiting in the fourth month, and was herself wasting away because it was so difficult to eat and drink. She was saved by her mother's faith and by St Stephen (*Miracles of St Stephen*, PL 41. 843–9; Brown 1981: 44). Puerperal fever is less dramatic but just as fatal: we do not know its incidence, but saints were invoked to calm it (Rousselle 1991: 322). Theodoret's mother, pregnant at last, survived a near-miscarriage in the fifth month by the help of Macedonius, and puerperal fever (of which her doctors despaired) by the help of Peter the Galatian (*History of the Monks of Syria* 9, 13; PG 82. 1387, 1410).

On the other hand, successful childbirth, producing too many children, could be a disaster for family property. Yearly pregnancies were a hazard of married life (John Chrysostom, *On Virginity* 55, PG 48. 577). Sidonius (*Letter* 2. 8) laments the death of Philomathia, who was scarcely 30, and left five children. Medical textbooks offer remedies both for infertility and for over-fertility, but there was great social pressure against the use of contraception or abortion. Contraception was necessary for prostitutes, who catered to men's sexual pleasures but could not demand that any one of their clients took a father's responsibility for their children. A wife was the woman selected to bear a man's legitimate children. It could, therefore, be argued that a man should not beget on his wife more children than he was prepared to raise, and that he was treating her like a prostitute (as we would say, a sex-object) if he used, or required her to use, contraceptive methods. This applied especially to oral and anal intercourse and to the various sexual postures believed to inhibit conception; the use of *coitus interruptus* is oddly difficult to document for any period of Graeco-Roman antiquity (Hopkins 1965a: 143–50). Detailed condemnation came later: penitential handbooks for priests begin to offer guidance from the mid-sixth century (Payer 1984), but until the eighth century there was no specific penance for the use of particular sexual postures (Noonan 1966: 121). But the use of any contraceptive method declared that what a couple—or one of them—wanted was sex, not children; whereas a decision not to raise a child could, perhaps, be seen differently, as an admission that the family could not cope with this child now.

Augustine, strong as always for the single standard, acknowledged that women were not necessarily the victims here: if the woman agreed to contraceptive practices, or engaged in them herself, she was treating her husband as if he were her (adulterous) lover (*On Marriage and Desire* 1. 15. 17, PL 44. 423–4). The motives of married women who wanted to avoid, or terminate, pregnancy, were always suspect. Philosophers conceded that poor people might be quite unable to rear another child; doctors acknowledged that pregnancy might threaten the mother's life, but they thought that the people who were prosperous enough to listen to philosophers or hire doctors ought to be able to control their desires and to make responsible choices about procreation. The philosopher Iamblichus, writing in the early fourth century, is particularly scathing about the care people exercise in breeding dogs or birds, and their casual, perhaps drunken, bringing into existence of human beings (*On the Pythagorean Life* 211–13).

Christian writers agree about the control of desire, and also argue that contraception takes the life of the child who would have been born. John Chrysostom says (*On Romans* 24. 4, PG 60. 626) that it is almost worse than homicide, since the victim never had a chance to become human; others use the term *parricidium*, murder of close kin. Caesarius of Arles reproaches women of his congregation for using contraception themselves, although they would object to their female slaves or tenants doing the same; in a letter to the clergy of his province, he declares:

Let no woman accept potions for abortion, or kill children either conceived or already born . . . Nor should women accept those devilish potions through which they would be unable to conceive.

Whatever woman does this should know that she is guilty of as many homicides as the number of children she could have borne. (*Sermons* 44. 2, 1. 12)

Appalling though this claim sounds, it has to be taken seriously. It does not mean that women are guilty of taking life if they do not have all the children they possibly can: it does condemn any attempt to prevent or terminate pregnancy. Caesarius makes no moral distinction between the two. This is partly because of the general disapproval of non-procreative sex; but it would also be difficult in practice to establish what exactly the woman had done.

Soranus finds it necessary to make a distinction (*Gyn.* 1. 19. 60) between contraceptives and abortives. Medical terminology may well have been confusing (as in the present-day medical use of 'abortion' for what most people call 'miscarriage'), and the techniques and medicines used for different purposes were often very similar. Women might be genuinely in doubt whether they were preventing conception, provoking abortion, or bringing on a delayed period by the use of an emmenagogue. In pre-NHS Britain, well within living memory (Holdsworth 1988: ch. 4; Secombe 1990), women who could not afford another pregnancy took monthly purges which they described as bringing on a period, and a whole range of 'something from the chemist' was believed to be effective in ending a pregnancy. In our day the 'morning-after' pill, and the technique of menstrual extraction, deliberately leave it unknown whether conception has occurred, and there is uncertainty whether the IUD works by preventing a fertilized ovum from implanting. The ancient world likewise accepted unclarity, without our option of finding out.

Hippocratic medicine held that, until the embryo was 'formed' and the mother began to experience foetal movement, there was only a process of conception going on. Interference in this phase therefore counted as contraception (Étienne 1973: 29–30). Christians could find support for this in the standard Greek translation of Exodus 21: 22–3, which defines the penalties for hitting a pregnant woman so that she miscarries: they are said to be less if the child is not 'formed' (Noonan

1966: 90; Dunstan 1990: 5–6). Nevertheless, several Christian writers declare that the distinction between 'formed' and 'unformed' foetus is not morally relevant; it would follow that contraception, in the sense of intervention during the first trimester of pregnancy, is no different from abortion. But official condemnation of contraception took some time: the first Church council to do so (Noonan 1966: 148–9) was Braga, in AD 572, which enlarged on a canon of Ancyra (AD 314) against abortion; penitentials lack explicit condemnation (Payer 1984: 34) until the ninth century.

But it might not be admitted that the termination or avoidance of pregnancy was in question. Books of remedies typically prescribe any given drug for a wide range of problems, or alternatively a wide range of remedies for a given problem, without clear guidance on quantities or preparation. For instance, when Oribasius (*Medical Collections* 14. 63–5) deals with insufficient menstruation and lactation, he offers a brief discussion (from Galen) of the imbalances which cause the problem, then a long list of remedies (from Zopyrus), most of which are simply names of plants or other items. Many remedies are prescribed both for delayed menstruation and for vaginal discharge; many are even more wide-ranging (Riddle 1985). Thus *phlommos*, according to the first-century pharmacist Dioscorides (4. 102), stops diarrhoea, deals with persistent coughs, toothache, and eyestrain, cures scorpion-bite, and dyes the hair blonde. The Anicia Juliana manuscript of Dioscorides includes the two varieties of Aristolochia. Greater Aristolochia (fos. 17–18), taken with pepper and myrrh, expels not only lochia (the heavy discharge of blood which follows childbirth) but menstrual blood and the foetus. The problem envisaged is no doubt a foetus which had died *in utero*; but we might be reminded of the various uses of a 'D & C'. Round-leaved Aristolochia (fos. 18–19) promotes menstruation, expels the foetus, and helps against asthma, hiccup, shivering, spleen, abscesses, and convulsions. What could you say to a woman who insisted that she had not known she was pregnant, or had only been trying to stop hiccuping?[7]

[7] As in Osbert Lancaster's cartoon shortly after 'the pill' came into general use: 'Sure, Father, an' I thought it was just an aspirin.'

Just how effective these remedies were is another question. Recent research tends to optimism about the contraceptive effects of asparagus, pomegranate, juniper, rue, pennyroyal, Queen Anne's lace, and several others (Riddle 1985, 1991). An even more optimistic account (Jacquart and Thomasset 1988: 91) suggests that many contraceptives 'must have worked very effectively by modifying the vaginal pH'. By contrast, one (unpublished) guess is that between 20 and 40 per cent of ancient remedies contain relevant chemical agents; but, given the uncertainties of identifying and preparing the ingredients, far fewer actually worked. As some are highly toxic (a problem known to doctors: Riddle 1985: 67–9), this is just as well. The Greek word *pharmakon* (like 'drug', and like Latin *venenum*: D. 48. 8. 3) can be used both for medicines and for poisons: a medicine is not a poison until it kills someone.

The word *pharmakon* can also mean 'spell' or 'charm'; and in all three senses it was associated with women. Women often supplied domestic remedies as they did food and drink, though it cannot be assumed (King 1991) that all nursing was done by women. Poison is a woman's weapon because she is not trained to handle weapons of war, and magic spells are the weapons of the weak; less drastically, diet was believed to have a great impact on fertility and potency (Rousselle 1988: ch. 11). 'Unoffical medicine', which allowed women to evade the wishes of men, was another factor in hostility to contraception and abortion. Again, it would often be difficult to prove that a particular result was intended. Basil's response to a request for advice is informative:

The woman who deliberately aborted is guilty of murder. Among us there is no distinction between 'formed' and 'unformed'. Here it is not only the one who was to be born who demands justice, but the person who conspired against herself, because women usually die from such attempts. To this is added the destruction of the embryo, another murder, at least in the intention of those who commit such acts. But their penance should not be extended until death, but be kept within ten years; and their [spiritual] healing should be judged not by the length but by the manner of their repentance. (*Letter* 188. 2, PG 32. 672)

Basil returns to the question of abortion while discussing wrong actions which have an even worse result than intended.

Even if someone prepares a drug for another reason, and it kills, we count that as voluntary. Women often do this when they try to put a love-charm on someone with spells and incantations, and also give drugs which obscure the mind. If these women cause death, even though they intended one thing and did another, they are still counted as voluntary homicides because they have meddled with forbidden practices. And women who give drugs to procure abortion are also homicides, as are women who take toxic drugs to kill an embryo. (ibid. 188. 8, PG 32. 677)

The danger to the reluctant mother was not only spiritual. Any medicine which was toxic enough to prevent, or interfere with, conception was likely to harm the mother as well as the unborn child. Soranus (*Gyn.* 1. 19, 60), who accepts that abortion may be necessary for very young women or for others whose life is at risk, advocates gentle techniques: medicines, pessaries, massage, warm baths. If these failed, the use of instruments was so dangerous that it was probably safer to wait for the birth. There were some relatively safe and effective contraceptives, such as pessaries of wool soaked in oil or vinegar. Attempts to use a 'safe period' were unlikely to succeed, since it was generally believed that peak fertility was at the end of the menstrual period. Soranus (*Gyn.* 1. 10. 36) says that some people deny this, but one should ignore them. The time midway between two periods was thus thought to be the least likely for conception. (This belief survived into the 1930s: Laqueur 1990: 9.) Augustine says (*Manichee Morals* 18. 65, PL 32. 1373) that the Manichees advocated the use of the infertile period, to avoid entrapping more souls in matter (i.e. begetting children)—they recommended abstinence after menstruation.

Spacing children by lactation was morally acceptable, and did not have to be described as a birth-control technique. Babies were thought to be influenced by the milk they drank, so the mother's was best, and intercourse during lactation was not advised because of the risk of pregnancy. Lactation by itself is not an efficient contraceptive unless the mother is giving six feeds a day, but combined with a social restriction on intercourse it can have a considerable impact on the birth-rate. Some other social constraints might restrict fertility. Gregory of Tours (*Miracles of St Martin* 2. 24, PL 71. 951) tells of a severely handicapped child whose mother finally admitted that he was conceived on a Sunday—but she had not ventured to kill him; and Caesarius of Arles (*Sermon* 44. 7) says that intercourse on Sundays or fast-days produces lepers and epileptics. We do not know how widely this was believed. There was also a belief (Hanson 1987) that an 'eighth-month child' could not survive: this exonerated both parents and doctor, because the duration of pregnancy could not be exactly calculated and a child who did not survive could be classed as born in the eighth month. But parents, sadly, do tend to explain neonatal problems by something they think they have done wrong.

3.6. Menopause

There is some evidence (Amunsden and Diers 1970) for the expected end of reproductive life. Aristotle thought (but on what evidence we do not know) that most women reach menopause about 40 but some not until 50, and that women over 50 do not bear children (HA 585^b3-5, *Politics* 1335^a9). Soranus (*Gyn.* 1. 4. 20) agreed in general, but added that some women do not reach menopause until 60, and (characteristically) emphasized the range of variation. Oribasius (*Medical Collections* 142) opted for 50, possibly 60, but noted that some women may reach menopause at 35—especially the overweight ones who are also likely to reach menarche earlier. This range is also given by Aetius (16. 4) and Paul of Aegina (*Epitome* 3. 60). As with menarche, we do not know whether they thought in terms of total cessation of periods, or the beginning of the process; and, since we have only formal medical terminology, we do not know how women saw 'the change' and its discomforts, or even whether they had a name for it.

   Medical opinion links up with legal and ecclesiastical decisions on celibacy (see above, Sect. 2.7). A law of 390 (CT 16. 2. 27) had required that deaconesses must be 60. This was the age, according to 1 Timothy 5: 9, at which a widow might be enrolled in the Church's official list: younger widows were not to be enrolled in case they brought disgrace upon the Church. Basil (*Letter* 199. 24, PG 32. 724) also thought 60 was the right age. By the mid-fifth century, there was a change. The Council of Chalcedon ruled (canon 15) that women might be deaconesses at the age of 40, and this is also the critical age in a law of Majorian (*Nov.* Leo and Maj. 6. 5, AD 458) which decreed that a childless widow under 40, 'while she is still of an age to bear children', must either remarry or, if she chooses celibacy, surrender her property to her kin or the State. It is not explicitly said that 40 is a safe age because a woman who reaches menopause no longer counts as a sexually active, and therefore a dangerous, being: but, given the association of menstruation and desire, the thought may well have been there. Alternatively, or in addition, there may be the practical consideration that a woman of 40 has probably completed her family, or is at least unlikely to start one: natural fertility declines (even in these days of fitness and healthy diets) from about age 30, and conception after age 45 is very unlikely. But there are exceptions:

We have been asked by the Bar at Caesarea whether, if a woman aged over 50 has given birth, such a child should be constituted the father's heir and succeed to the inheritance. We rule that, although such a birth is remarkable and rarely happens, yet nothing which is (within the bounds of probability) produced by Nature should be rejected. (Justinian, CJ 6. 58. 2, AD 532)

Justinian decided that deaconesses should not be ordained before the age of 50 (*Nov.* J. 6. 6, AD 535)—and women were not eligible if they had been married a second time, something he regarded (*Nov.* J. 2. 4, AD 535) as a pardonable failure to resist the heat of nature.

3.7 Alternative Life-Styles

This is, perforce, a very short section. Graeco-Roman culture offers almost no information (Boswell 1980; Lardinois 1989) on female homosexuality at any period. The very few

references—with the great and much-debated exception of
Sappho—assume that female homosexual activity is in addition
to, or in emulation of, man–woman intercourse. Caelius
Aurelianus mentions 'the women who are called *tribades*
because they engage in both kinds of intercourse, are more
eager to have intercourse with women than with men, and
pursue women with an almost masculine jealousy' (*On Chronic
Diseases* 4. 9. 132–3; Drabkin 1951: 901–2). There are some
problems with the text; but the context is the 'disease' of men
who prefer the passive role in man–man intercourse, and the
tribades appear to be women who likewise try to assume a male
role. Medical texts include an operation for clitoridectomy, to
be undertaken when the clitoris is greatly enlarged and, 'some
report' becomes almost masculine (Paul of Aegina, *Epitome*, 6.
70; Hanson 1990: 333), but they do not make a connection with
tribades.

Christian texts too are generally silent on the subject, and
miss the opportunity to comment on an obscure remark in
Romans 1: 26–7 which might refer to female homosexual
intercourse. (One exception is the uncanonical Apocalypse of
Peter, which includes in those consigned to Hell 'women who
lay with women as with men': Rousselle 1991: 359.) There are
a very few references in penitentials (Payer 1984: 138), with
some mention of 'instruments' used to simulate man–woman
intercourse. Perhaps any less macho activity was unknown
to, or ignored by, men. In the Middle Ages (Jacquart and
Thomasset 1988: 159–60) female homosexuality was thought
to be less serious than male homosexuality because no loss
of seed was involved; besides, it was supposed that woman–
woman intercourse occurred as a substitute where there had
been no satisfaction from man–woman intercourse. So far as I
know, Bremmer (1989: 46) is right to conclude that a Lesbian
identity was not an option in late antiquity.

3.8. Female Complaints

It seems only too likely that many women suffered the consequences of child-bearing: 'wives with bodies broken through

pregnancy's dire curse, through birth's hard labours' (Ephraim the Syrian, *Hymn* 8. 8; trans. Brown 1988: 330).

Most women have a hateful time in the world. They give birth in pain and danger, they suffer in breast-feeding, when their children are ill they are ill too. They endure this without any end to their hard work. Either the children they conceive are maimed in body, or they are brought up in wickedness and plot to kill their parents. We know this: let us not be deceived by the Enemy into thinking that way of life is easy and trouble-free. When they give birth they are damaged by labour, and if they do not, they are worn down by reproaches of barrenness. (ps. Athanasius, *Life of Syncletica* 42, PG 28. 1511)

John Chrysostom (son of a woman widowed early, and himself unmarried) observed the general effects. Married men, he says, have unrestricted intercourse with their wives: this reduces their desire. 'And besides this, birth pangs, parturition, the bearing and rearing of children, and prolonged sicknesses which, with their after-effects, besiege the body, cause the bloom of youth to fade, and produce a diminution of the sting of pleasure' (*Against those men cohabiting with virgins* 1, PG 47. 496; trans. E. A. Clark 1979: 166). Virgins, by contrast, are still vigorous and attractive at 40—which is why it is very dangerous to cohabit in supposed chastity. As if that were not enough, women made themselves ill with worry when their husbands were away (*On Virginity* 57, PG 48. 578).

How much could be done for ailing women? The problems which loom largest in the medical texts, other than menstrual and reproductive difficulties, are haemorrhage and vaginal discharge. Anaemia, and diseases transmitted by the sexual freedom of husbands, are very likely to have occurred, but successful diagnosis is unlikely. It is difficult now (Grmek 1988) to identify sexually transmitted diseases which may have been prevalent; but it seems clear that, when husbands were warned against infidelity, no use was made of the argument that they might infect their wives or their children. Medical texts also failed (Rousselle 1988: ch. 4) to connect general physical problems with frequent child-bearing.

The commonest medical problem of antiquity seems (Jackson 1990: 12–13) to have been eye infections. Theodoret's mother first consulted the holy man Peter the Galatian because a lady recommended him for eye trouble (Theodoret, *History of the Monks of Syria* 9, PG 82. 1382). The problem most often submitted to saints, apart from infertility, was demonic possession (Harvey 1990: 117–18). Reports of healings emphasize the spectacular cases which occur in the Gospels—paralysis, blindness, deafness, expulsion of demons—but also mention fevers and fertility problems.[8] Gregory of Tours reports fevers (in one case leading to blindness), chills, dysentery, a woman with contracted tendons and another with swollen and crippled hands (*Glory of the Confessors* 58, 95; PL 71. 870, 899). There were also breast cancers. Peter the Galatian was able to dissipate the pain of one young woman, but not to cure it (Theodoret, *History of the Monks of Syria* 9, PG 82. 1385). A woman known to Augustine (*City of God* 22. 8, PL 41. 763) was told by her doctor that she would live longer if she did not submit to surgery. No doubt many surgery patients died from shock. The treatment of pain (H. King 1988) included some painkilling drugs, but (from what Augustine says of other cases of divine healing) they had little effect on the pain of the operation. Syncletica, a desert saint, died apparently of cancer, which affected her lungs and her mouth; the smell was so bad that her attendants could scarcely bear to come near her. She allowed a doctor to use myrrh, aloes, and myrtle dipped in wine to treat the sores, but only for the sake of those with her.

Drought, famine, and epidemics afflicted the entire population, but women may have been especially vulnerable to contagious diseases which caused death or miscarriage (Patlagean 1977: 89, 99). Their use of the public baths certainly exposed them to water-borne infections (Scobie 1986), since people used the baths particularly when they were ill. Abstinence from baths was a sign of sanctity because it demonstrated unconcern for the body, and this too must have caused health problems. Not going to the public baths, for the sake of modesty, is one thing; not washing is quite another. Olympias rarely went to the baths, and when persistent stomach trouble forced her to do so, she did not bathe naked (*Life of Olympias*

---

[8] Adnès and Canivet (1967), Patlagean (1977: 103–12), Rouche (1987: 457–8).

13; E. A. Clark 1979: 138). In a treatise ascribed to Athanasius, the virgin is exhorted:

Do not go to the baths, if you are healthy, without great need; do not immerse your whole body in water, for you are consecrated to the Lord. Do not defile your body with anything worldly, but wash only your face, your hands and your feet. When you wash your face, do not use both hands, or rub your cheeks, or apply herbs or nitre or such: worldly women do that. Wash in pure water. (PG 28. 264)

She was also told to take care of herself (PG 28. 264–5) in case anyone said she was ill because of her ascetic practices. This was an understandable suspicion: no wonder Roman gossip ascribed the death of Blesilla, a young woman not long married, to her extreme asceticism in widowhood (Jerome, *Letter* 39. 6, PL 22. 472).

Melania the Elder, according to Palladius (*Lausiac History* 55), reproved a deacon who, at the end of a gruelling journey, washed his hands and feet. She was all of 60, she said, and she had washed only the tips of her fingers. Perhaps she, or Palladius, exaggerated. But her fellow-aristocrat Paula (according to Jerome, *Letter* 108. 20, PL 22. 897) said that a clean dress was the sign of an unclean mind, and Paula's prescription for desire was more rigorous fasting. Dirty and underfed, women saints must have had more health problems than the ulcers and lice which are mentioned as patiently borne, or the spectacular physical suffering which brings honour to the ascetic. Augustine took a firm line about proper care of the body, with baths when they were needed (*Rule for the Servants of God* 9, PL 32. 1383; Lawless 1987: 115–16); and he added, for the benefit of nuns (*Letter* 211. 13, PL 33. 963), that they should have their usual bath once a month, and more often if it was advisable, without complaint.

4

DOMESTICITY
AND ASCETICISM

HOUSES and housework are a subject on which we need, more than ever, texts written by women. Domesticity was the female role, and men, having defended or merely asserted this basic point, took little further interest in it. It had been argued since the fourth century BC that staying at home is not just a social convention. Women, it was said, are physically suited to staying home just as they are to child-bearing, and households need the division of labour in which the man goes out and the woman stays in. In practice, the traditional task of 'looking after the household goods' included all kinds of money-making activities, from small trade (especially in fabric) to property deals (Huchthausen 1974, 1976).[1] A group of Egyptian Christian women, Didyme and 'the sisters', seem to have had an all-female network buying and selling wine, grapes, sandals, cakes, even a purple-wrapped ostrich egg (Emmett 1984; Wimbush 1990: 462–3). But what did women actually do in the house?

The immediate problem is that men (at least, men in the writing classes) either did not know in any detail, or did not see fit to say more than general comments on, the role of women—mistress of the house, bailiff's wife, female slaves—in the household. There is an interesting contrast here with the (perhaps artificial) precision of the Mishnah (Wegner 1988: 76–7), which specifies a woman's duties as grinding corn, baking, and laundering; preparing meals and nursing her children; making her husband's bed, and working wool. For each slave she brings in her dowry, she may omit one set of tasks, in the

[1] More information will be available from a database, compiled by Suzanne Dixon of the University of Queensland, on the economic activities of women in the Roman empire.

order stated—but R. Gamaliel thought she must continue to work wool for fear of idleness.

Graeco-Roman writers described either the great and prosperous houses which (like the English country house) were far more than a family home, or, at the other extreme, the poverty of the destitute or of the voluntary ascetic (Patlagean 1977: 55–67). The middle range did not interest them; or perhaps they did not have much relevant experience, for even the clergy, who might be expected to show concern for the living conditions of their people, were severely criticized if they visited women at home. Nuns and deaconesses did visit women, but did not (of course) write about it.

It is difficult to discover what houses at any social level were like in terms of spaces and surfaces, rooms and their uses, and what needed doing to keep them presentable. There is nothing like the eighteenth century 'housekeeper's books' which show how much routine maintenance was required for a gentleman's house and its furnishings. Perhaps modest households had less in the way of furniture and fabrics than a twentieth-century western housewife would expect: pegs rather than cupboards and wardrobes, tiled or mosaic floors rather than carpets, chairs without cushions, simpler bedclothes. Some evidence is provided by the bequests of household goods made in (later) Byzantine wills (Oikonomides 1990). As always, higher social status meant more household goods, and especially more fabrics—tapestries and carpets—to cover walls and floors. The self-professed Christian magistrate denounced by a Pelagian treatise (*On Riches*, PL suppl. 1. 1386) lolls on a heap of elaborate drapes as he orders torture and execution. At any social level, general standards of cleanliness may well have been lower than they are today. Even so, it seems likely that somebody had to sweep the floors, polish the wood and metal, clean up the wax-stains and the smoke-stains from the braziers, or at least make sure that the slaves were doing it properly.

Again, there is information on what people ate (Patlagean 1977; 36–53; André 1981), but not on how they cooked it. Poor people might not get cooked food at all, unless they were taken into a Christian hospice where the care provided would include hot food and fresh bread (Patlagean 1977: 47). Grains and pulses can be made edible by soaking rather than cooking; vegetables can be eaten raw. But bread, when it could be afforded, was a basic foodstuff; and, even if bread was bought from the baker, some cooking would have been needed in ordinary households. Unfortunately, no one tells us about it. Gregory of Tours (*Glory of the Martyrs* 80, PL 71. 776–7) has a splendid account of a special effort made by one woman to entertain her own Catholic priest and her husband's Arian adviser. The Arian blesses each course as it comes in, so the Catholic will not eat it; but the Arian chokes to death on an obviously familiar dish, a kind of omelette garnished with rounds of grapes and olives (identified by Brown (1981: 81) as *omelette á la provençale*), which has been brought to table sizzling hot in the pan in which it was cooked. But what was the heat source? A charcoal brazier, or an open fire with trivets and an oven beside it, like a kitchen range?

Excavations provide town plans and sometimes ground-plans of individual houses, but so far these have not revealed much about practical matters like kitchens. The problem is that, as a rule, only foundations survive: there is very little in the way of wall-decoration or of furniture, unless it is a marble table (Ellis 1991: 123–4). Baths and latrines are easier to detect, and perhaps we can deduce an increasing concern for personal privacy from the liking for private baths and the subdivision of interior space by corridors and partitions (Ellis 1985: 20; Thébert 1987: 391–2). But it would be risky to generalize from the evidence. In the Greek east (Rossiter 1989) not many houses have been excavated; the majority of those that have are town not country houses, and their building plans are not always complete. We have, of course, to allow for differences of local tradition as well as of class. For instance, grand African houses (Thébert 1987: 325–6) do not follow the Roman tra-dition of an *atrium*, an open-roofed entrance hall beyond the main entrance which is used for the reception of visitors and also by the family, and which gives access to the *tablinum*, the office or study of the master. Instead, great houses in the provinces generally have peristyle courtyards which are differently related to the house as a whole. They do indeed give access to the most elaborately decorated room in the house, the formal dining-room (*triclinium* or *oecus*), but visitors might never be admitted to the courtyard: they could be sent down a corridor to a reception room (Ellis 1991: 122). In northern Syria (Sodini and Tate 1984) the blank outer wall of the house is pierced by a main entrance which leads to a courtyard, but here the courtyard is for farm animals and equipment, and the family rooms are in the upper storey.

Differences of scale, again, may do more than enlarge: country villas, like Piazza Armerina or Melania's estate at Thagaste, almost amounted to private towns (Macdonald 1986: 274), with their own bath houses and churches. The Thagaste estate was bigger than the nearby town; it included many craftsmen in precious metals, and two bishops—one for Catholics and one for Donatists. Another of Melania's properties had sixty-two households grouped round a spectacular bathing-pool, with views over the sea to one side and a wood with wild animals to the other (E. A. Clark 1984: 40, 190).

Imagination can be helped by representations of townscapes and interiors, but there are few of these, and there is nothing like the loving detail of a 'Dutch interior' or a medieval nativity. Literary descriptions of great houses, as in Gregory of Nyssa (*Letter* 20, PG 46. 1080–5), or Sidonius' account of an estate brought to him by his wife (*Letter* 2. 2), focus on their grandeur and on such amenities as private baths and fountains, not on everyday life and organization. The house described by Sidonius, who devotes much more space to the bathing-rooms than to anything else, includes a dining-room for the ladies next door to the storeroom and the weaving-room (ibid. 9); a separate room for 'nursemaids and dependent females' to eat in at times when they will not disturb the family (ibid. 11); and two formal dining-rooms, one for winter and one open air for summer (open-air dining was fashionable: Rossiter 1991). The house of one of his friends (ibid. 2. 9) had an improvised sauna for use until the baths were finished. When Sidonius visited it, guests met before lunch in the library, where some discussed books and the less intellectual played board games, before moving to the *triclinium* for the meal.

On the evidence we have so far, it is easier to determine how private houses were related to the public facilities of the town than to decide what it was like to live and work in one of them. The most promising area of research is on the divisions of private and public space within the great houses, which had always functioned as centres of business and political activity (Thébert 1987, with several house plans). Ceremonial rooms are conspicuous by their mosaic floors and often by their shape. The fashion was for curved dining-couches (*stibadia*), with round or semicircular tables, which were set for preference in a curved space, perhaps a 'triconch', a three-apsed room next to a larger square room for entertainments (Ellis 1991: 119; Rossiter 1991). At the other extreme, the slave quarters may be detectable. But it is much more difficult to distinguish any areas in a house which were particularly 'women's territory' (cf. A. Wallace-Hadrill 1988).

Bedrooms can sometimes be identified by a platform for the bed, or a change in the pattern of the floor tiles where the bed is to be placed. Dining-rooms too may have bays or platforms for dining-couches, or there may be white panels in a mosaic floor where the couches were to be placed. But when bedrooms open off a courtyard or are placed next to a dining-room, they may be guest-rooms rather than family rooms. Besides, the divisions of space were not necessarily permanent. Rooms could have different uses, bedding and storage-chests could be moved as built-in wardrobes cannot, curtains and removable doors could modify space. In the visual arts, a curtain probably indicates 'privileged space' which was not open to all comers. Smaller private houses might provide separate sleeping quarters, but (according to John Chrysostom) it was quite possible for a man to blunder out in a state of undress into a room full of women (*That women under rule should not cohabit* 8, PG 47. 529).

4.1. Denouncing Housework

It may seem paradoxical that the best sources of information on housework are treatises on virginity. These aim either to persuade women that domestic life is drudgery, or to persuade men that they do not need a wife to look after the house.

Jerome, arguing that marriage really is a spiritually inferior form of life, presents the harassed housewife:

Over there the babies are prattling, the children hang on her for kisses, the accounts are being added up, and the money got ready for payment. Here a posse of cooks, girded for action, is pounding meat, and a crowd of weaving-women chattering. Then a message comes that her husband has brought his friends home. She circles the rooms like a swallow: is the couch smooth? Have they swept the floor? Are the cups properly set out? Is dinner ready? Tell me, where in all this is the thought of God? (*Against Helvidius* 20, PL 23. 214)

Pelagius, writing to another lady (*To Celantia* 24, PL 22. 1216, there ascribed to Jerome) was characteristically strong-minded about the housewife who claims she has no time to pray or read her Bible. It is, he says, a matter of setting aside time each day. But the most interesting excuses came from people who said they were celibate but still shared a household. Why, John Chrysostom asks (*Against those men who cohabit with virgins* 9, PG 47. 507), should a man who lives a celibate life want to take a celibate woman to live with him? Does he perhaps have foreign slave-women who need training? Does he want someone to take charge of the storeroom, to supervise expenditure and make sure things do not go missing, to prepare banquets and decorate the house and organize cooks and waiters? The male celibate is imagined as replying that, on the contrary, he wants someone to manage his household chest, look after his cloak, set the table, make the bed, light the fire, and wash his feet. Washing cloaks, making fires, and boiling pots, according to Chrysostom himself, are skills that women have but men must learn (*That women under rule should not cohabit* 4, PG 47. 520). But he makes the obvious reply that monks appear to manage without help. A woman, by contrast, might argue that she needs a man not for his domestic skills, but to represent her in conflicts with officials, rivals in business and in the family, or disrespectful slaves (*Against Remarriage* 4–5, PG 48. 615–16; cf. Ambrose, *On Widows* 9, PL 16. 264–5).[5] Evidently Chrysostom is thinking in terms of a household with slaves, for he does not suggest that some physical tasks might be beyond her strength.

Responsibility for the household goods, 'keeping the keys',

while the man of the house is about his public business, was an essential part of the female domestic role. A little girl 'playing house' would have her own little chest in the storeroom, and keep the key (*On Virginity* 73. 1, PG 48. 586). The unmarried woman does not have to worry about money, slaves, stewards, property, cooks, weaving-women, and so on (ibid. 75, PG 48. 588–9). Apart from this managerial role, the typical female task was making fabric. It was immediately obvious when a celibate man shared a house with a woman: there on pegs would be women's shoes, belts, headbands, baskets, a distaff, 'things for weaving' (*Against those men cohabiting with virgins* 9, PG 47. 507). But still there was no need to have a woman in the house to make cloth, for many women sold their work. They usually marketed it themselves, and could use an old woman or a slave-girl as agent if they did not want to stand in the market-place. In Chrysostom's eyes, a male cohabitant might become embarrassingly feminized, going around to workshops on his partner's errands and picking up the characteristic speech of women chatting over their work. Eventually he will be quite unable to talk of anything but woolwork, and the effect on his character will be deplorable. He will be just like a woman: at once servile and insolent, mean and extravagant, feeble and reckless—in short, a cowardly lion (cf. E. A. Clark 1986: 26). On the other hand, he may run the household, and then the woman is no freer than if she had married (E. A. Clark 1986: 183).

John Chrysostom envisaged an oddly limited selection of domestic tasks. He grew up with a widowed mother who had slaves; he lived for a time with other male celibates, but never married. When he was bishop of Constantinople, his meals were provided in the house of Olympias. He appears to have the consumer perspective on housework, combined with what is now known as 'learned helplessness'. When he is not advocating celibacy, he is quite prepared to argue for traditional role-division, on the grounds that men are just as incompetent at housework as women are at public business. This, he says, is a blessing: otherwise women would be despised if men could do housework, or would be unbearably conceited if they themselves did housework and public business too (*The kind of women who should be taken as wives* 4, PG 51. 230). A woman can spin and weave and do all the other household tasks (unspecified); she can bring up children and keep the servants in order; she frees her husband from concerns about the house, money, woolwork, and the provision of food and clothes.

The philosopher Hierokles (quoted by Stobaeus: 4. 28. 21) seems to have a wider—though still conventional—understanding of household chores. Perhaps he had (or inherited) a rural perspective. Women, Hierokles says, generally do woolwork, make bread, and cook, but some physically demanding tasks might well be done by men. (This does not include woolwork, which is done only by very poor specimens of manhood.) He instances grinding corn, kneading dough, cutting wood, fetching water, carrying large containers, and shaking out covers. Women can also make bread, light fires, draw water, make beds, and help with farming and harvesting, at least to the extent of handing the farmer tools as he needs them. But Hierokles is working in a tradition which emphasizes the common human nature of men and women and the duties they share; and perhaps he is, after all, less realistic than Chrysostom in taking a peasant household as the domestic model for the high-minded.

4.2. Minimizing Housework

Something more can be deduced from the living arrangements of women who had cut household duties to the minimum in order to lead the ascetic life. Women were not encouraged to lead a solitary life in the desert, where they were themselves in physical danger and also posed a spiritual threat to the monks, the 'Desert Fathers' who were trying to escape from desire and from the pull of human social life: a few achieved it. The reported sayings of Amma Syncletica, one of the few 'desert mothers', were included in various collections (Ward 1975) which circulated in the fourth and fifth centuries. They make use of domestic imagery from the role she had rejected.

Just as sturdy clothes, trodden and turned in washing, are made clean and white, so a strong soul gains in strength by voluntary poverty. But those souls which have weaker reasoning power experience the opposite. Even if they are only slightly pressed down, they are destroyed, like clothes which are torn: they cannot stand the washing given by virtue. (ps. Athanasius, *Life of Syncletica* 30, PG 51. 1505)

It is like people who want to light a fire: at first they are affected by the smoke and weep, and so they achieve what they want. Scripture says 'Our God is a consuming fire', and we must kindle the divine fire in ourselves with tears and hard work. (ibid. 60, PG 51. 1523).

Women ascetics were urged to create their own 'desert', a place free from the demands of the world, within their own home or in a house shared with other women. This is perhaps how the widowed Marcella overcame the hostile Roman reaction (Jerome, *Letter* 127. 5, PL 22. 1089) to what was seen as a degrading life-style. When Athanasius and others told her about the Alexandrian ascetic discipline, she pioneered it in her own house, living with her mother and instructing her aristocratic women friends. Her household included Asella, who lived enclosed, working with her hands and praying, and Lea, who stayed in her own room and received disciples. In Syria, Domnina (Theodoret, *History of the Monks of Syria* 30, PG 82. 1492) lived in a hut in her mother's garden. Remaining at home was not recommended for ascetic men (Jerome, *Letter* 125. 11, PL 22. 1078), since their mothers would insist on feeding them properly, and the slave-girls would be a constant temptation. (Melania's mother also tried to persuade her daughter to relax the severity of her Sunday fast, but failed: *Life of Melania* 25.)

If one important woman in a household took to the ascetic life, her women relatives, dependents, and slaves might join her, so that the household became a community. Basil's sister Macrina never married, and never left her mother. She led the ascetic life at home for some years before her mother was free to join her, having discharged her worldly duties; their slaves followed suit, and they took in some girls whom they had rescued from famine (Gregory of Nyssa, *Life of Macrina* 11, PG 46. 969). The women slaves of the widows Paula and Olympias, and of the virgin Demetrias, likewise followed the example of their mistresses; so did the household of Caesaria the Patrician (Harvey 1990: 127–8). But this household model created problems. Ascetic women might be called *canonicae*, women living under rule, but in the fourth century they were pioneers: there was in fact no established rule of life for ascetic households, and individual ascetics could invent their own. It is a recurrent theme in advice to communities that people from different social backgrounds have genuinely different needs and powers of endurance: those who need, for instance, greater care when ill should not be despised. In a strongly hierarchical society, social barriers loomed as large as practical problems. The Christian humility of the great ladies concerned had to come to terms with their social status (E. A. Clark 1986: 175–228). Caesarius of Arles, drawing up rules for nuns almost a century later, feels bound to specify that not even the Superior may have a personal maid (*Rule* 7).

Part of the solution was for the ladies to join in domestic tasks which had been considered servile, especially kitchen work. Palladius found a story (*Lausiac History* 34; K. Vogt 1987) of a female 'fool for God', a member of the Pachomian convent at Tabennisi whose bizarre conduct proved to be motivated by her sanctity. She showed her humility by insisting on staying in the kitchen doing menial tasks, even when it was not her turn. It must have been even more impressive when women of high status took their turn at the chores. Macrina made her mother's bread with her own hands, and there were no social distinctions in her household (Gregory of Nyssa, *Life of Macrina* 11, PG 46. 969). Paula and her daughter Eustochium shared in the preparation of vegetables—but in their community at Bethlehem women of different social status ate separately. On a much smaller scale, Marana and Cyra lived with their former servants, who had their own hut (Theodoret, *History of the Monks of Syria* 29, PG 82. 1489–92).

Woolwork was easy to integrate into the ascetic life-style. Women of all classes learned to make fabric, and it was traditionally an activity of the virtuous domestic woman. The monks of Egypt used the weaving of palm-leaf baskets to occupy the hands and leave the mind free for prayer. Weaving wool could do the same, and Jerome (*Letter* 130. 15, PL 22.

1119) advised Demetrias to make fabric for use or sale, the proceeds to be given to the poor. Alternatively, women could make clothing to be given directly to the poor. The household of Pulcheria, sister of Theodosius II, wove fabric instead of spending time in amusements (Sozomen, *History of the Church* 9. 3, PG 67. 1604); the holy women Euphemia and her daughter Maria supported themselves and some poor people by selling cloth, Maria weaving and Euphemia marketing her work (Harvey 1990: 123).

In an ascetic community, the woolwork could become too much of a preoccupation. Augustine's rule for monks and nuns provided for some members of the community to be in charge of clothing, which was to be held in common (*Rule for the Servants of God* 8, PL 32. 1382; Lawless 1987: 114–15). Basil (*Shorter Rules* 153, PG 31. 1181) required a sister in charge of woolwork, and Caesarius (*Rule* 27) pointed out that the Superior had to be free from concerns about woolwork, which were therefore to be delegated. Most rules for ascetic communities were designed to apply both to men and to women— with the proviso that women would need even more decorum, submissiveness, community feeling, and caution about meetings and about movement outside the community (ps. Basil, *Second Ascetic Discourse* 2, PG 31. 888a). Alternatively, the rule for a community of men was minimally adapted for women (Elm 1991: 120), much as it was in girls' schools and women's colleges in the late nineteenth century. This sometimes had the effect of changing the traditional assignment of tasks by gender, but sometimes, where there were double communities of monks and nuns, the time-honoured role-division continued, with suitable precautions against meeting. In the Egyptian communities founded by Pachomius, the women looked after the clothes and the men did the heavy digging and food-production (Elm 1987: 167–72): in effect, this was an economically successful village in which the sexes did not cohabit. Basil's *Rule*, which is in fact a set of responses to questions from communities, covers the problem of a small group of m onks who work for a larger group of nuns, and who cannot always stay together (*Shorter Rules* 154, PG 31. 1184). But Caesarius (*Rule* 36) allowed no men to enter the convent—with the exception of a priest to say Mass or work-men to do building repairs.

4.3. *Clothes and Dress Codes*

One of the standard criticisms of women, rooted in tradition and repeated in endless patristic sermons, is the time and effort and money they spend on their appearance: clothes, jewellery, hair, make-up. This is, notoriously, an area of misinter-pretation between the sexes, and what we read about is how men saw women. Almost certainly this is also what we see in the visual arts. There may have been women artists—painters, mosaicists, illustrators of manuscripts, carvers in ivory or even stone, workers in precious metals who made medallions and caskets and dishes—but from Pliny in the first century to Vasari in the sixteenth century no one troubled to write about them (Chadwick 1990: ch. 1). Textiles were predominantly women's work, as other art-forms were predominantly men's, but most textiles have perished. We can see, and read, that clothes were enriched with gold thread, heavy embroidery, narrative panels which were themselves miniature works of art, but only small samples survive (Monnas and Granger-Taylor 1989; Bowersock 1990: 52–3).

So, as usual, we are working with the 'male gaze', but that is not the only problem. Late-antique art does not set out to report how women actually looked. It is difficult to read even the kind of image—fashion drawings and photographs—which is designed to tell us about clothes: sometimes it is impossible to imagine why anyone would be prepared to dress like that. But the women's clothes portrayed in late-antique art are usually in the category of drapery, that is, fabric being used by an artist for the line, movement, bulk, exposure, or whatever else it gives in relation to the body which it drapes. The artist draws on the vocabulary of artistic tradition, not on the vocabulary of the clothing worn in his time.

'Classical drapery' has been so prevalent in European art that classicists tend to think of it not as clothing but as an aspect of Greek or Roman art, and classical art historians have mostly used the portrayal of clothes and hair-styles to demonstrate the style of a particular artist or (especially in Roman sculpture) as a dating criterion. It is not a very good dating criterion for fashion, even when we can tie a particular portrait to a particular named woman (Holum 1982: 41–2), precisely because artists reused styles; late imperial female portraits (Smith 1985: 221) tend to follow second-century models. Thrifty owners also reused statues, fitting a new head to an old body or even replacing a stone wig.

But drapery does, at least, tell us that the artist chose to present the subject draped in such a way, and possibly the artist's choice interacted with the subject's perceptions of what she looked like. Work on fashion and images, in the 1970s and 1980s (Hollander 1975; Lurie 1981), alerts us to what the cloth does in relationship to the body, which areas of the body are emphasized or downplayed, what message the clothes convey about the person wearing them. There is much more expert work to be done on using this approach to the clothes of Graeco-Roman antiquity: classicists have, perhaps, been put off by all the years in which clothes, hair-styles, and marriage ceremonies made up most of the content of any writing about women. But relevant work is beginning to appear both on images and on textiles (Mills 1984; Geddes 1987; Granger-Taylor, forthcoming).

4.4. *The Image of Theodora*

The most famous visual image of a woman from the later empire is a mosaic in the church of San Vitale, Ravenna. It shows the empress Theodora, among her court ladies, opposite Justinian and his courtiers. Where statues may repeat a 'classical' convention, this is a contemporary image of an empress. The clothes she is wearing (and those of her attendants) could not successfully be conveyed in sculpture, partly because of their line, but chiefly because of their strong colour and detailed ornament. Her imperial purple cloak has a deep border, probably embroidered, which shows the Magi (themselves richly dressed in Persian style, and wearing predominantly red) bringing their gifts to Christ, and her collar and headdress are heavy with jewels of many colours. Vividness and variety of colour is one of the most striking features of late Roman art. This might be an accident of survival rather than artistic preference: we have far more mosaic, in relation to uncoloured stone and faded fresco, than in earlier periods, and the mosaicist's technique (Onians 1980) works best with several colours and with detailed ornament. But, in a different medium, late Roman poetry (Roberts 1990) also reveals a taste for contrasted colour and for varied formal arrangement.

The mosaic portrait of Theodora is quite startlingly different from the images of royal women of the earlier empire. We can scarcely talk of drapery: the fabric does not drape the underlying body, which is only a prop for the cloak falling almost straight from its heavy jewelled collar. Like the cloak, the body is vertical. The body does not curve, the fabric is not held in at the bust or the waist, and the vertical line below the yoke, emphasized by the vertical stripe, is modified only by the heavy border at the hem. Only the face and hands of the woman underneath are visible under the layers of clothing.

Deliberate layering of clothes is often an indication of wealth. By contrast, the woman wholly or mostly exposed is socially unprotected. One of the mosaics of the villa at Piazza Armerina in Sicily shows women gymnasts, who wear only bikinis; Theodora herself, in her early stage career, is said to have worn even less (Procopius, *Secret History* 9. 1–30). Alternatively, the naked or near-naked woman is too grand to think of her slaves as observers (Brown 1988: 315–17). Perhaps reaction to sexual exploitation or arrogance, as well as extreme anxiety not to provoke desire, is a factor in Christian standards of modesty.

Do not strip naked; let your garment cover your flesh night and day. Let no other woman see your body naked, unless in great necessity, and do not be aware of yourself with body unclothed. From the time when you resolved to be chaste for God, your body was sanctified and is God's temple. God's temple must not be uncovered by anyone. (ps. Athanasius, *Treatise on Virginity* PG 28. 264)

But Theodora's clothing, though it hides her body, is not like the protective *chadur* which aims to make its wearer socially invisible. Her face is not only visible, but emphasized by its frame of jewellery and head-dress lifting up from the forehead. The two women nearest to her have folds of their cloaks drawn over their heads, the others are apparently bareheaded. (When Melania went to see Serena the wife of Honorius, at Rome in the early fifth century (*Life of Melania* 11), court etiquette required an uncovered head.) But formal hair-styles—assuming that sculptors and moneyers represent them accurately—are so structured that they hardly look like hair. It looks as if the hair was parted in the centre and taken back into a plait or into several braids. The front strands are waved. The plait may be taken back up to the crown of the head, or, if it is long enough, wound round in a circlet.[2] This 'towering hair' (*turriti crines*) is part of the standard account of the 'vain woman'. Male writers do not say whether their objection is to the time taken, or the claim to status, or attempts to improve on nature by hair-pieces and pads and dyes and waving. The beautiful Eudocia, formerly Athenais, wife of Theodosius II, had curly blonde hair (Holum 1982: 114): if this was the ideal, Mediterranean ladies had problems.

It is, as always (MacMullen 1980), difficult to assess how much veiling of hair or face was expected of ordinary women. Augustine tells his sister's community of nuns that their hair should be covered, and not with something thin enough to show their hairnets. They should not be seen outside the house with their hair either loose or carefully styled (*Letter* 211. 10, PL 33. 1181). A decisive commitment to celibacy was symbolized by *velatio*, formal veiling. Ambrose (*On Virgins* 1. 65–6, PL 16. 218) describes a young woman rushing to the altar and declaring that its cloth shall be her veil—better than the *maforte* (see below) of the nun or the *flammeus* of the Roman bride. The metaphor 'bride of Christ' was taken very seriously, but veiling connoted modesty as well as marriage. Holy women were praised for keeping their heads covered and their

---

[2] Examples in von Heintze (1971), L'Orange (1973), Holum (1982: 32–4). LaFontaine (1970: 58–61 discusses hair-styles, and other aspects of dress, described by Prudentius.

gaze lowered, so that they never looked a man in the eyes (see below Sect. 5.2). It was no use for radical celibate women to argue that they need not veil, because they were liberated from femaleness: those who saw them were not liberated from maleness.

The empress was a visible public figure, not a modest matron. In modern terms, Theodora is engaging in power-dressing, both in clothes and in body language. She has the strong shoulders and the straight vertical line, unmodified by the soft or wavy hair which declares that the modern executive is sexy too—unless (Barber 1990) her tall jewelled crown, with its strands of gems dangling over her jewelled yoke, has a similar feminizing effect. The crown, its shape emphasized by the niche above it, gives her extra height; and her clothes (like the modern executive suit) are an adaptation of a male uniform. The other women wear the *palla*, a lightweight cloak like a large shawl, which is variously draped across the upper part of the body. Theodora wears the *paludamentum*, the imperial purple cloak. Its deep embroidered border, which shows the Magi bringing gifts to Christ, emphasizes that she too is a royal person bringing gifts: she carries a chalice for use in the communion service.

But there are important differences from the presentation of her husband the emperor, as well as conscious similarities (Holum 1982: 30–4; Smith 1985: 215). Justinian's diadem is far less imposing: it can afford to be, because he wears the full imperial uniform. His shoes are purple and his cloak is fastened with the official *fibula*. He is in the open, escorted by identifiable high officials and bishops, whereas Theodora and her ladies are passing from one enclosed space to another—probably the interior of a church, so they have an excellent reason for being temporarily in public view (MacCormack 1981: 260–4; Barber 1990).

Theodora's clothes are not peculiar to royalty. With the exception of the imperial cloak, they are one variation on what, from the evidence of art, is standard late-antique clothing for women. The long, straight tunic, the *dalmatica*, varies in width, but not to the extent of being pleated or gathered like the classical Greek chiton or the early imperial stola. Its line is severely vertical, often emphasized with a central stripe or a panel of embroidery or woven design. It can also be tied in under the bust or the waist. The very different effect of a narrow tunic tied at the waist is shown in another Ravenna mosaic, the procession of female martyrs in Sant'Apollinare: here is the beginning of the sinuous medieval body outlined, rather than hidden, by fabric. There can also be a strong horizontal line at the hem, provided by a decorated border on the tunic itself or on the cloak or underdress. The tunic is high-necked and the neckline is emphasized with jewellery, ranging from a simple one-strand necklace to the imperial splendours of Theodora: again, there is a great difference from the loose, baggy necklines of earlier clothes. The arms are not usually exposed: the underdress has close-fitting sleeves to the wrist, and the tunic has shorter, wider sleeves above. Tight sleeves, according to Jerome (*Letter* 130. 18, PL 22. 1122), are provocative—though it may not be unfair to say that, to Jerome, any item of clothing that fits is provocative, including shoes (see below, Sect. 4.5). Altogether, these are clothes, sewn or shaped to fit, not draped cloth.

Over all this the cloak can be draped in many ways. Theodora's is vertical and its border hangs down her right side, so there is no interruption of her imposing stance. But a cloak can be front-opening with two bands, giving width and verticality: usually the dress underneath hangs straight, without a belt. It can also be swathed with great fluidity and complexity, or can simply cover the wearer without sending any signals about the body.

The basic components of late-antique dress are constant, but they can be arranged to make different effects. We have no way of detecting changes in fashion—for instance, colour, weight of textile, where to position the borders; provincial ladies may have rushed to copy the hair-style of the latest imperial portrait (Smith 1985), but it is much harder to show what they did about the clothes. But what we can perhaps do is look at the 'reception' of clothes: that is, the kind of signals which men thought were being sent, and women were (perhaps) aware of sending. The language of clothes involves the listener as well as the speaker.

4.6. *Clothing as Language*

The men who wrote about women's clothes did so in the general and moral terms that had been current since Hesiod described Pandora, the first woman. What they do not do is to denounce women's clothes in some sort of interesting detail. James Laver, the historian of costume, interpreted fashion in terms of a Seduction Principle for women and a Hierarchical Principle for men. But, if we are to believe the male writers of late antiquity, women's clothes combined the two: by expressing status they attracted attention, and it appears to be taken for granted that such attention (if male) is lustful. Consequently, gold and jewels, purple and embroidered silks, elaborate hair-styles and make-up are deplored for the benefit of women who probably had little chance of affording them, or who had no intention of buying them in the first place. It depends, of course, on the audience envisaged (MacMullen 1989). Jerome and John Chrysostom, who were contemporaries, use very similar language to denounce women's efforts to adorn themselves; but John Chrysostom is concerned about the waste of money which could have been spent on the poor, and Jerome (as usual) is worried about sexuality (E. A. Clark 1979: 58–9).

Some patristic denunciations are drawn straight from the Bible, repeating attacks on Babylonian arrogance of the sixth century BC or on the women of Asia Minor in the first century AD (I Timothy 2: 9). This does not mean that they are stereotypes without relevance to practice. We complain that the 'massive continuities' of women's lives are too much taken for granted, but purple and gold and fine linen and elaborately styled hair were also there to be denounced in the later empire, because they were still the obvious manifestations of wealth. Clothes were valuable things. The ransom demanded by Alaric the Goth in 411, when he held Rome, included silk tunics and scarlet fleeces. Sosiana, widow of a *cubicularius* (an imperial chamberlain), gave the church embroidered silk clothes worth a pound of gold each, and linens with designs in the weave, and clothes enriched with gold thread. These were to be used as altar-cloths and veils: she gave orders that they should not be

sold for the benefit of the poor, in case a prostitute got them
(John of Ephesus, *Lives of the Eastern Saints* 55).

There are clear indications of the styles and fabrics which
demonstrated wealth and status, or conscious renunciation of
wealth and status. The ancient world (unlike our own) was able
to define such status-indicators with some hope of success,
in cultic regulations (Mills 1984) or sumptuary laws (Culham
1982, 1986). In the later empire (CT 15. 7. 11–12, AD 393–4),
actresses could be forbidden to dress so that they looked like
nuns, or, alternatively, too much like members of the royal
house. Multi-coloured silks and plain gold jewellery were
allowed; jewels, embroidered silks, and fabrics enriched with
gold, and a particular dye which in some lights looked like
purple, were going too far.

Purple is the most famous status-indicator (Reinhold 1970:
ch. 6): to be precise, one particular grade of purple which from
Constantine on came to be associated with the imperial family,
so that anyone who used it illegally could be suspected of
an intended *coup*. True purple was expensive as well as eye-
catching. The exact colour-range of purple is a problem, as
with all colour-words from antiquity: dyes were not stable
(Onians 1980), colour-groupings might be quite different from
ours, and colours certainly made different impacts at different
times. But purple had a long history at Rome. In the second
century BC the Greek historian Polybius noted the status-
coding of Roman senatorial dress in terms of purple and gold,
and Livy was probably right to interpret the third century BC
debate on the lex Oppia, which had forbidden women to wear
these things, as concerned with women's status-claims and bid
for power (Culham 1982).

Another status-indicator is silk, which was probably im-
ported until the sixth century and was in any case very expensive to produce (Muthesius 1989). There were less expensive
'mixed' fabrics, and there were different weights and textures
of silk. Diocletian's edict on prices includes half-silk underwear
with purple stripes. (This edict as a whole is informative on
grades of clothing, textiles, and their manufacture in the late
third century, but not, of course, on how they looked.) Other
prestige fabrics were the finest grades of linen and wool, often

from named areas (the equivalent of Cashmere). Silk, wool, and linen could be enriched with gold thread, which was woven into fabrics or used in the very complex designs which decorate some clothes, like the Magi on Theodora's cloak (Maguire 1990) or the panels which denoted an official rank. Jewels were also used to decorate clothes, with a preference for strongly contrasted colours (Roberts 1990). Jewellery as such, (*monilia*), was an important part of family property, like a tiara for the British aristocracy: the primary meaning of *monilia* seems to be the heavy necklace worn at the high neckline of the tunic. Women intending to be deaconesses were required to give their jewellery to the family, not the Church (CT 16. 2. 27, AD 390; see above, Sect. 2.7.). Jerome tells us (*Letter* 127. 4, PL 22. 1089) that the saintly Marcella, at her mother's wish, reluctantly gave hers to her rich relations instead of to the poor; and (ibid. 130. 7, PL 22. 1113) that the heiress Demetrias, who made a spectacular choice of virginity, owned enough jewels in her own right to make married women envious.

Christians who chose the ascetic life abandoned their embroidered silks (Patlagean 1977: 54). A few went to the extreme of near-nudity in rejecting corrupt human civilization, like Mary of Egypt (Brock and Harvey 1987), but most opted for the clothing of the poor, who might have only one garment and certainly lacked a range of possibilities for warmth and cleanliness. It is unexpected to find 'contemptible clothes' in a list of the virtues of Olympias (*Life of Olympias*; 13; E. A. Clark 1979: 137), but we must take it seriously: such clothes proclaimed low status, as clothes could do in Britain until the advent of chain stores. The 'reverse' status-indicators for late antiquity are coarse cloth and absence of colour or decoration. This does not mean white, but black.

White was symbolic of purity, and therefore was used for baptismal robes, as it had been in older traditions. According to Iamblichus (*On the Pythagorean Life* 153), the followers of Pythagoras imitated his dressing in clean white linen, like the initiates of the Mysteries; they banned black because it did not show dirt, and russet because it did not show blood-stains. But who was going to wash all that clean white linen? Pythagoreans were an aristocratic group. Christians who renounced the world wore black precisely because it connoted dirt and deprivation: it was the colour of mourning, and poor people wore dark clothes. Black, worn by the ascetic, said 'I am a poor sinner.' Nuns, it appears, were not actually required to wear black. Augustine is concerned chiefly that his sister's community should wear simple clothing, and should hold it in common so that the sisters should not become attached to a favourite dress. (This rule, like all Augustine's rules for a monastic community, applied also to monks: Lawless 1987: 114–15.) Caesarius of Arles actually forbids either black or shining white: 'just a plain, decent colour' (*Rule* 44), *laia* or *lactina*, literally 'milky', which probably means unbleached cloth. It was a symbolic change of clothing, not a uniform, which marked the transition to the ascetic life, and Caesarius' nuns had to wait a year to make it.

It is interesting, in this context, that multi-coloured clothing, as worn by those like Melania's son (Paulinus, *Letter* 45. 3, PL 61. 393) who had not 'changed their clothes' for ascetic dress, could still have a positive symbolism. In Platonic tradition white is pure, simple, unmixed; *poikilia*, varied colour or decoration, is elaborate and multiple. In the first century AD the Stoic Epictetus envisages the wise man as the single purple stripe which transforms the look and significance of a plain garment (he is thinking of the formal dress of a Roman senator). But Ambrose, in the fourth century, interpreted Joseph's coat of many colours as a symbol of his manifold virtues (Schwarz 1973; McHugh 1976).

Absence of colour and ornament had to be reinforced by texture. Coarse cloth might be made of goat's hair: this is *cilicium*, the original hair shirt. Some grades of it were used for tents. There was also camel's hair, as worn by John the Baptist, which, to judge from a thank-you letter of Paulinus of Nola (*Letter* 29. 1, 5; PL 61. 312, 315), was even more exquisitely uncomfortable. (His return gift was a lambswool tunic, which no doubt heaped coals of fire upon the sender's head.) In the same letter Paulinus describes the elder Melania returning from the Holy Land to sort out her family, and provides a vivid picture of the significance of clothes. All the relatives, dressed (men and women both) in their embroidered wools and silks,

came to meet her at Naples, their carriages causing a traffic-jam
on the Appian Way—and there was a little woman in shabby
black.

The *Life* of the younger Melania (E. A. Clark 1984), ascribed
to the priest Gerontius, uses clothing as an indicator of her
progress in holiness. In her early married life (*Life of Melania* 4)
she was already wearing a tunic of coarse wool under her all-
silk robes, and was much upset when her aunt found out. (This
aunt was lucky. Jerome (*Letter* 107. 5, PL 22. 873) tells us that
Praetextata, aunt of his favourite Eustochium, tried to smarten
up her ascetic niece's hair and was punished by fatal illness.)
Melania then used the death of her second child as a reason for
abandoning silk (*Life of Melania* 6). Her own near-death in
labour had persuaded her husband to join her in asceticism
(ibid. 8). She wore a cheap, used *himation* (an all-purpose garment) to efface her youthful beauty; he wore Cilician clothes,
but was still showing concern for his appearance, so she
talked him into wearing undyed clothes from Antioch. The
'Cilician clothes' were evidently not the haircloth *cilicium*:
perhaps they were made of Cilician linen (E. A. Clark 1984:
189), which was not top quality, but good enough to worry
Melania.

Melania then insists (*Life of Melania* 11) on wearing her
'garments of salvation', which include a veil over the head, for
a visit to the empress: court etiquette at Rome required an
uncovered head. But she does take silk clothing among her
presents for court officials. Later (ibid. 19) she and Pinianus
offer their remaining silks at the altars of churches and
monasteries, where they were probably used as altar-cloths. In
her monastery, Melania wears day and night, between Easter
and Pentecost, a *himation*, scarf and hood of haircloth—and this
although her sensitive skin, in childhood, was inflamed by the
embroidery on a linen dress (*othonê*). The scarf (*maphorion,
maforte*) protected the head and neck; it was worn by women as
a head-covering, and could also hold the top of a loose
monastic tunic in place to free the arms for hard work (Cassian,
Institutes 1. 7, PL 49. 72). When her uncle met her in Constantinople, and saw her cheap, poor clothes, he grieved at
the remembrance of the gently-nurtured child (*Life of Melania*

53). She was buried wearing a sleeved tunic (*sticharion*), a scarf, a girdle, part of a sleeveless tunic, and a hood, all of which had once belonged to other saints and carried some of their sanctity; she was wrapped in a simple winding-sheet (ibid. 69).

The treatise on virginity ascribed to Athanasius (PG 28. 264) gives detailed instructions on dress and its significance.

If you do not dress in youthful clothes, you will not be called 'young woman': you will be called 'old lady' and treated with respect as an older woman. Do not let the material of your clothes be expensive. Your cloak should be black—not dyed, but naturally so—or onyx-coloured.[3] The scarf should be the same colour, without tassels. The sleeves should be woollen, covering the arms to the fingers; the hair cut short, with a woollen headband tied round the head, and a hood, and a shoulder-covering without tassels. If you meet a person, let your face be veiled and downcast: do not raise your face to a human being, but only to God. When you stand to pray, let your feet be covered with shoes, for this kind of clothing is suitable for holiness.

The typical virgin (John Chrysostom, *On Virginity* 7, PG 48. 537–8) had messy hair, downcast eyes, and a dark cloak, as recognizable as the cloak and staff of the wandering philosopher. But even this outfit had possibilities, and Jerome was peculiarly sensitive to them. As he points out to the sister of a worried Gallic monk (*Letter* 117. 7, PL 22. 957), a cheap dark dress could be wrinkle-free and floor-length to make the wearer look taller; it could have strategically placed rips showing tantalizing glimpses of flesh; a bra and tight belt lifted the bust; the hair was not pulled back, but hung down from the forehead or over the ears; the shawl just happened to slip off the shoulders; black shoes could be polished, and creaked to attract attention. The effect was not that different from the ways of girls openly out to attract, with their make-up and their hair 'let down from the forehead', their tight sleeves and their smooth dresses and their low necklines and their shoes that fitted closely (ibid. 130. 18, PL 22. 1122). There was also the pseudo-virgin with a purple *maforte* floating about her shoulders (ibid. 22. 13, PL 22. 402). Poor people evidently could not afford clothes, or shoes, that fitted.

[3] There seem to be two possibilities for onyx-coloured clothing: black with white flecks, like Arabian onyx; or white.

Jerome distrusted feminine charm, but also objected (ibid.
22. 27, PL 22. 413) to those who tried to deny their female
nature by cutting their hair short and dressing—as Melania
did—in *cilicia* with hoods. Little children wore hooded cloaks
too, he says, but these eunuch-faced women peered out like
owls. Perhaps this reaction explains why nuns in Pachomian
communities did not wear the monastic cloak (Palladius,
Lausiac History 33). Thecla, role-model for aspiring women
ascetics, had dressed as a man to travel in search of Paul (*Acts of
Paul and Thecla* 40), but that, evidently, was in the dangerous
old days. Jerome was not the only one to be shocked. The
Council of Gangra (probably mid-fourth century: Wimbush
1990: 27) had denounced women who cut their hair and dressed
like men; and a law of 390 (CT 16. 2. 27. 1), regulating the
conduct of women who have opted for the ascetic life, declares
that those who have cut their hair short may not enter
churches, and if the bishop allows them in he is penalized. A
few cases of cross-dressing were reported with approval (see
below, Sect. 5.2) because they were safely hidden in the desert,
and because the women concerned were trying to hide the fact
of being female, so that they could lead a strict ascetic life,
rather than to deny the code of femininity.

So Theodora can dress in a style very much like that of
her husband, but deliberate 'masculinization' is improper. The
ideal, according to Christian writers, is a style of dress which
does not attract attention either by its splendour or by its osten-
tatious poverty (Jerome, *Letter* 22. 27, PL 22. 413). Women, it
appears, were always concealing their true appearance, whether
by make-up and fashion, or by negation of their sexuality
(Averil Cameron 1989: 189). There is a fine (but unhelpful)
declaration of principle in Augustine's letter (262. 9, PL 33.
1081) to Ecdicia, a lady who had decided to renounce the
world without actually consulting her husband.

It is written that women ought to wear a well-regulated dress; adorn-
ing with gold, and twisting the hair, and all that sort of thing, which
leads to empty display or seductiveness, is rightly rebuked. But there
is a style of dress appropriate for a married woman and distinct from
that of a widow, which can be suitable for faithful wives without
detracting from religion.

Your husband, says Augustine, prefers that you should not look like a widow while he is still alive; and you should obey him with shining white conduct rather than resist him with black clothes. Theodoret's mother, though married and aged only 23, renounced fine clothes, make-up, and jewels on the orders of Peter the Galatian (*History of the Monks of Syria* 9, PG 82. 1383); Gorgonia, sister of Gregory of Nazianzus and also a married woman, did likewise (*In Praise of his Sister Gorgonia* 10, PG 35. 800). Both were praised for it: either they got the balance right, or they were lucky in their male relatives.

BEING FEMALE

FEMALENESS, by general consent, was a disadvantage. It was assumed that females were physically weaker than males, were unlikely to be the intellectual equals of males, and had a more difficult time controlling bodily desires and the onslaughts of emotion. This was held to be true even if they escaped some of the dangers of femaleness by choosing virginity, or if they were trained in philosophy and became the respected partners of philosophic men. On this question we do not suffer from the usual shortage of evidence: we are very well informed about the dominant ideology.

Graeco-Roman philosophers could usually forget that what they wrote about moral choices and life-styles was not relevant to women, for their students were young men, and they often taught in public places where women did not go. If any women were present at their lectures, perhaps in private houses, they were the daughters or wives of men who were themselves part of the philosophic group (see below, Sect. 5.3). The philosopher could take for granted that his audience thought women should be given the same moral training as men, but not the same education in gymnastics and rhetoric; they might be just as capable of virtue as men, but should exercise their virtue in the traditional life-style of the wife and mother. A brief and—in that setting—uncontroversial discourse would settle the question.

But Christian philosophers could not escape so easily. Even solitary ascetics were pursued into the desert by women's anxieties and illnesses, and the Church hierarchy had to deal with women all the time. When Augustine (or John Chrysostom, or Basil) was a layman, he could discuss philosophy with a male peer-group. As a bishop he had to preach to a congregation of women (probably the majority) and men, deal with the pastoral problems of women both married and celibate, and keep on good terms with the rich and powerful women who were major benefactors of the Church. He had to expound a revealed text which described the creation of woman and the redemption of the world by a saviour born of woman, and which authorized both the maintenance and the rejection of the social norms which governed women's lives.

Consequently, we find much patristic discussion of the nature of women and the way women should live. But, inevitably, we know very little about the responses of anyone not in the male educated élite. Did women internalize the perception of themselves as weak and inferior beings? Were these assertions simply 'protocols', things which people felt they had to maintain in public, whatever they really knew about competent women? How many people were seriously concerned about whether women had the same reasoning power as men, or were made, like men, in the image of God?

5.1. *Inferiority*

The physical differences between male and female could be explained by the relative weakness and coldness of the female. These had their practical uses in reproduction, but were nevertheless a proof of female inferiority. But human beings were held to be not only body, but soul: the soul is the reasoning power which differentiates humans from other living creatures. It enables us not only to reason, to make sense of the world, but to understand what is good and to do it undistracted by other desires. God is pure reason and pure goodness; the more the human soul is devoted to wisdom and undistracted by the body, the closer a human being is to God.

This belief was common to Christian and non-Christian philosophers, with the difference that the Christians recognized a profound wisdom in people who were by human standards quite unintellectual, but whose life of prayer and renunciation made them intensely aware of God. (Some of the Desert Fathers, for instance, were illiterate, or had no knowledge of Greek or Latin to connect them with the culture of their admirers: E. A. Clark 1986: 198.) There were further debates about the immortality of the soul, about reincarnation, and especially about what Christians call grace. Can the soul, trained by self-discipline and hard study, approach God by its own powers, or must we suppose that God assists the process? So there was also a question whether the soul of a woman is, like her body, weaker than that of a man, and less capable of intellectual and moral attainment.

Aristotle had argued that it is. The female body differs from the male because it has a lower level of vital heat. This must also affect the female power of reason, which never reaches full development in the female, any more than menstrual blood is ever sufficiently heated to become semen. Women cannot, therefore, be expected either to match the intellectual ability of the male or to have their reason fully in control of desire: they need external guidance and restraint to stay out of trouble. This was a reassuringly scientific explanation for common prejudices, which remained in full force among those who had never heard of Aristotle.

Platonists and Stoics disagreed: they argued that women may have more to contend with, and *qua* female are obviously inferior, but men and women share a common human nature and aim at a common excellence (*aretê*). So women's souls are not as such inferior to the souls of men, and if properly trained they are just as capable of manifesting virtue. The Christian consensus too (Waszink 1947: 420) was that the soul is not sexed. Christians believed that God created human beings in God's own image—and God is not limited by human categories, including the categories of male and female. If woman, like man, was created in the image of God, then woman must have the rational soul which is the most Godlike aspect of humans, and her physical weakness is no excuse for moral failings. The point is strongly made in a homily on Genesis which is probably by Basil of Caesarea (Horowitz 1979: 195); it is reinforced in other writings of Basil, Gregory of Nazianzus, and Gregory of Nyssa (Gould 1990).

But some Christian philosophers debated a further problem. Genesis 1: 26–7, in Greek or Latin translation, declares that God created *anthrôpos* or *homo* in God's own image: male and

female God created them. Both *anthrôpos* and *homo* mean
'human being'. Greek and Latin have other words (*anêr* and *vir*)
for male human being, and do not allow the confusion caused
by the English use of 'man' both for 'male human' and for
'humankind'.[1] Basil (*Homily 10 on the Six Days of Creation*, PG
30. 33) took the trouble to refute a possible objection by
women that, because the Greek text uses the masculine article
with *anthrôpos*, only male humans are meant: Scripture, he
says, excludes this mistake by adding 'male and female he
created them'. But, if God is not sexed, why are there two
sexes of human being in God's image?

Gregory of Nyssa (*On the Making of Humanity* 16–17, PG
44. 182; Floeri 1953) produced an ingenious suggestion that
Genesis 1: 27 actually describes a double creation. Humans are
a compound of divine and animal nature: the divine element is
the rational soul, which God created first in God's own image,
without distinction of male and female. So it is possible to say
that in Christ, the prototype of God's image, there is neither
male nor female (*Gal.* 3: 28). The distinction between male and
female animal nature, in the second half of the verse, was God's
provision for reproduction, since God foreknew that human
beings would fall into sin; being thus distanced from God, they
would be unable to multiply as the angels do, neither marrying
nor giving in marriage. It follows from this line of argument
(Gould 1990: 6) that women do not need to transcend or negate
their femaleness.

A simpler solution was to read Genesis 1: 26–7 in the light of
Genesis 2: 17–25, which describes the creation of Eve from
Adam's rib. Modern feminist exegesis points out that, in the
Hebrew text, *adâm* means the human being created by God:
there is no male Adam until 'the *adâm*' is separated into male
Adam and female Eve. But, even with this emphasis, it is the
male human being who keeps the name of the original creation. Patristic writers found it natural to assume that the normative human being was a man, just as they found it natural to
speak of God as masculine even though they affirmed that

---

[1] This usage, unfortunately, survives: it ought to be an archaism. The only thing
to be said for it is that (like referring to God as 'he') it conveys the androcentrism
of patristic writing.

God was not constrained by human categories. So, although Eve was flesh of Adam's flesh, the same kind of creature (Theodoret, *Questions on Genesis* 30, PG 80. 127), having a rational soul like him, and although Adam was incomplete without Eve, woman was a secondary creation for the benefit of man. This made it easier to interpret Paul's assertion (in the course of his attempts to convince the women of Corinth that they ought to wear veils, *1 Cor.* 11: 7) that man is the image and glory of God, but woman is the glory of man. Lactantius, for instance, evidently found it quite straightforward: 'when He had first made the male in his own likeness, he then also formed the female in the image of the human being [Latin *homo*], so that the two sexes together could produce offspring and populate the earth'. (*Divine Institutes* 2. 13. 1, PL 6. 319; Perrin 1981: 416).

Augustine (*On the Trinity* 12. 7, PL 42. 1003–5) did not find it straightforward at all: there appears, he says, to be a contradiction between Genesis and the Apostle (Paul) on whether woman is in the image of God. His solution is like that of the Platonists and Stoics: woman considered separately, as helper (Gen. 2: 8), is not in God's image, whereas woman considered together with man, or man considered separately, is in God's image. He makes a comparison with the human mind, which is God's image when it contemplates truth. When part of it is contemplating truth, and part is diverted to temporal concerns, it is God's image only in the part which contemplates truth. The bodily veiling of women, as being not in God's image, represents the part of the mind which is directed to temporal things—though of course women can contemplate eternal truths just as men can. There is a similar suggestion in the *Confessions*, as Augustine reflects on the glories of creation:

Just as in the human soul there is one part which rules by making decisions, and another which is subordinate and obeys, so woman is in bodily relation to man: she has the same nature as regards rational intelligence, but in bodily sex is subject to the male sex, just as the impulse for action is subject to the intelligence, to receive from it expertise in acting rightly. (*Confessions* 13. 22, PL 32. 866)

So the interpretation of Genesis reinforced the common belief: women have rational souls like men, but they are physically associated with weakness, irrationality, and animal nature more than men are. One example among many is Origen's allegorical interpretation (*Homilies on Exodus* 2, PG 12. 305) of the Pharaoh's instruction to the Israelite midwives to kill the male babies and let the females live. 'I have often shown, in discussion, that in women the flesh and the desires of the flesh are symbolized [in the biblical text]; man is rational awareness and intellectual spirit.' Hence Pharaoh's instruction symbolizes a wish to destroy the rational soul and let the flesh triumph. Unfortunately, both the Greek word for 'desire' (*epithumia*) and the Latin (*cupido*) are feminine nouns, as are the names of many specific desires: it was too easy to personify them as seductive females. So it seemed obvious that man is the normative and prior creation, and the subordination of women to men is required by the creation of woman as a help for men. John Chrysostom is thus able (*Homily 8 on Genesis* 1, PG 53. 72) to dismiss any suggestion that 'image' can mean 'bodily form': that would mean that God is like a subordinate being, woman, which is impossible. (Feminist exegesis inverts the argument: since the Hebrew word *ezer*, translated 'help', is also applied to God, it cannot imply subordination.) Augustine illustrates natural subordination (as opposed to the social hierarchies of a fallen world) with the examples of corporeal to spiritual, earthly to heavenly, female to male, irrational to rational, less worthy to nobler, more restricted to more comprehensive (*Literal Interpretation of Genesis* 8. 23, PL 34. 390).

Why, then, was this inferior kind of human created? The obvious answer is that women are differentiated from men so that reproduction can occur. The emphasis here could be that, in effect, a woman is a man with internal not external reproductive organs. Instead, we find it argued that the only reason for women being there at all is for reproduction. Augustine considers the question in *Literal Interpretation of Genesis* (9. 5, PL 34. 396): what is meant by saying that the woman was created as a help for the man (Gen. 2: 18)? If Adam had wanted help to cultivate Eden, another man would have been stronger; if he was lonely, another man would have been better company. Perhaps the problem was that another man would have refused to acknowledge Adam's leadership? But he would have known himself to be the second created. The only help that a woman could give better than another man is in reproduction. Nevertheless, Augustine decided (*City of God* 22. 17, PL 41. 778), women would not in the resurrection become men (as some people deduced from Eph. 4:13), for God had made both sexes.

John Chrysostom could see an objection to virginity (*On Virginity* 14, PG 48. 543): if there is no marriage and child-bearing, what is the use of women? When persuading men to virginity (ibid. 46–7, PG 48. 567), he declares that women are more of a hindrance than a help, except as regards the arrangement of this present life, child-bearing, and sexual desire—unless, of course (ch. 47), they are a spiritual help. When arguing against the remarriage of widows (*On Remarriage* 4, PG 48. 615) he takes a different line: many widows are perfectly competent (as his own mother had been), and God said 'Let us make man a helper' to stop him being conceited and thinking he could manage by himself.

Sexual differentiation, then, is for reproduction. In *City of God* (14. 21–4, PL 41. 428–32) Augustine speculates on what reproduction would have been like if humans had not disobeyed God and been made subject to desire: he envisages a conscious choice to procreate, obeyed by the genitals, without the swamping of the rational mind by orgasm and without damage to the female body (see above, Sect. 3.3). It is the narrative of the Fall, in Genesis 3, which adds the finishing touches to the subordination of women: 'In sorrow you shall bring forth children, and your desire shall be for your husband, and he shall rule over you' (3: 16): painful childbirth, sexual desire despite the risks of child-bearing, domination by a husband, are Eve's punishment for listening to the tempter and giving Adam bad advice.

John Chrysostom's *Homilies on Genesis* are a particularly revealing set of reflections on this story. He envisaged God saying to Eve, 'I created you, in the beginning, equal in honour; it was my wish that you should have equal status with him in everything, and as I entrusted rule over all things to the man, so I did to you' (*Homily 17 on Genesis* 3, PG 53. 144). Eve was created subordinate to Adam but like him in every way:

complete and perfect, rational, able to give help. She threw away her advantages in typically female fashion. She had no business talking to a snake (who was, in any case, one of her servants, since God gave humans dominion over the earth) when she could have talked to her own husband; and Satan approached her because it is always easier to deceive women. Because Eve's advice was bad, women are permanently barred from giving instruction: step down from the professor's chair! Yet even in punishment God's mercy is seen. It is actually better for women to be kept under control, just as it is better for a horse to be reined in than to be free to plunge over a cliff. Women suffer in pregnancy and childbirth but experience joy at the birth of a child; they forget the pain and are willing to go through it all again. Even the lordship of their husbands can be pleasurable for them; though, Chrysostom muses, male headship does not always work out quite as God intended. As his audience knew, not all men succeeded in ruling their wives.[2]

5.2. The Legacy of Eve

A Christian woman had the option of refusing the role defined for her by society and Scripture. She could argue that Mary's obedience to God had redeemed the disobedience of Eve; that Christ had redeemed all the children of God from slavery to sin, and that she too was a baptized Christian who had Christ's help in resisting sin. Her physical weakness could be overcome, and she had the moral and spiritual strength to manage without the support of a husband; she could resist desire and refuse to bear children in pain; she would be choosing the better part by devoting her life to God, as the bride of Christ, as a chaste widow, or even (with her husband's agreement) in a celibate marriage.

So a Christian woman could achieve respect by rejecting the claims of family, by devoting herself to the study of theology, and even by travelling on pilgrimage to sacred places and martyr-shrines and holy ascetics, walking among people from

[2] cf. E. A. Clark 1979: ch. 1 for the evolution of his approach; Pagels 1988 for an extended contrast of John Chrysostom and Augustine.

whom she would usually keep her distance on mule-back and with an escort (Brown 1981: 43–4), if indeed she was prepared to be seen in public at all; Justinian's legislation makes provision for women who are not used to any public appearance (Beaucamp 1990: 137–8). Gregory of Nyssa was moved to warn the intending pilgrim of the dangers and discomforts of travel (Hunt 1982: 70–1). It was, of course, much easier if she had contacts: the pilgrims Melania the Elder, Paula, Silvia, and Poemenia (and probably Egeria, who stayed for some time at Constantinople) had friends at court and among bishops (Hunt 1982: 76–82, 159–56). Perhaps only Bishop Atticus, preaching in Constantinople in the presence of Pulcheria, sister of Theodosius, could go so far as to declare: 'Through Mary all women are blessed; the female can no longer be held accursed, for the rank of this sex surpasses even the angels in glory. Now Eve is healed . . .' (Holum 1982: 141); and he went on, anticipating the feminism of the 1970s, to list the admirable women to be found in the Bible. But Ambrose too (*On Widows* 9. 51, PL 16. 263) could use Biblical heroines to prove that women cannot use their nature as an excuse, or widows plead the weakness of their sex and their need for a husband's support.

The social pressures remained. Virginity (Averil Cameron 1989) was liberation from the demands of society, but also control of desires which might arise in the celibate woman or those whom she met. A fourth-century homily on virginity, addressed to the father of a family, goes so far as to urge him to keep his 'prisoner' safe from the dangers of vigils, assemblies, and funerals.[3] As we have seen, female ascetics were still expected to follow the patterns of modest domesticity, venturing out only with safeguards, and their appearance and manner was a rejection of desire. Mary's obedience had countered Eve's disobedience (Graef 1966), but that did not mean that Eve's daughters could now think themselves exempt from female failings, any more than they could bear children without pain. Mary had said what she ought in response to God, whereas Eve had assented to evil; but it did not follow that Christian women could now give public instruction or exercise

---

[3] Text in de Mendieta 1953, tr. Teresa M. Shaw in Wimbush 1990: 33–44.

leadership. The Apostle (Paul) had said, 'I do not permit a woman to teach' (1 Tim. 2: 12) and teaching was acceptable only in private and with due regard for the proprieties, including deference to men (Nürnberg 1988: 66–73).

When the learned Marcella answered questions on exegesis, Jerome reports approvingly, she gave the credit to Jerome himself or to some other man, 'lest she should seem to injure the male sex, or sometimes even priests' (*Letter* 127. 7, PL 22. 1091). There is an interesting divergence in the Greek and Latin versions of the *Life of Melania* (E. A. Clark 1984: 22–3) on Melania's challenge to Nestorianism at Constantinople. In the Latin life she exhorts noble women to constancy; in the Greek, her audience includes men of learning. But private discussions with a distinguished Christian woman were not preaching. It was still a man's task to go out and spread the word, because women have less resolution in proclaiming the word and are weaker in following it (Ambrose, *Exposition of Luke's Gospel* 10. 157, PL 15. 1937). Women were prominent in many theological movements which came to be seen as heretical (Van Dam 1985: 74–7, 100–1; E. A. Clark 1986: 33–7). Their status within any such movement was one way of attacking it, on the grounds that women are naturally more credulous than men, and that it is quite improper for them to be in authority. If Mary did not baptize or exercise priesthood, it could not be right for other women to do so (Epiphanius, *Medicine-Chest against Heresies* 79, PG 42. 743; an argument which has survived). Mary herself became an example of poverty and modesty (J. Vogt 1974: 163–8) even while cities invoked her protection as queen of heaven (Averil Cameron 1978, 1979, 1991). It could only be the Devil who inspired two monks with a vision of Mary enthroned, surrounded by angels who demanded that they worship her, ordaining them priests. When the vision faded, the girl seated on the throne proved to be one of those waiting for exorcism (Harvey 1990: 119).

Christian teachers agreed with non-Christians that a woman can manifest courage, the virtue whose name in Greek or Latin actually means 'manhood' (*andreia, virtus*); but she should fight a solitary battle against sin in the privacy of her room, not make an unsuitable foray into public life (John Chrysostom to Olympias; *Letter* 6, PG 52. 599). And a woman who had triumphed over female weakness was praised—as Olympias was and many others were—not for being a brave woman, but for being a man. Amma Sara, one of the very few 'desert mothers', lived alone by the Nile for sixty years, never allowing herself to look at the river; for thirteen of those years she struggled with sexual temptation. Two monks decided to humiliate her: 'Be careful not to become conceited, thinking to yourself, Look how anchorites are coming to see me, a mere woman!' She replied, 'According to my nature I am a woman, but not according to my thoughts. . . . I am a man, and you are women' (Ward 1975: 193).

There is a recurrent story of the woman ascetic who, made unfeminine by fasting and concealed by the monastic habit, joins a community of monks or lives as a hermit assumed to be male; she passes for a eunuch to explain why she need not shave, and is detected only when her body is prepared for burial (Anson 1974; Patlagean 1981). The most famous of these 'transvestite' saints was the reformed prostitute Pelagia (Brock and Harvey 1987). This form of sanctity went out of fashion by the ninth century, but, at the time when the stories were formed, the modesty and resolution of the saint made her behaviour admirable rather than outrageous. Nevertheless, she was not an example for all to follow, and she was safely away from public view in the desert. Femaleness as such was still a cause of shame, even if the solitary woman took refuge in the very deepest desert with the wild creatures, away from all risk of human contact. The classic case is Mary of Egypt (Brock and Harvey 1987), who is finally seen by Zossima the priest, naked, hardly recognizable as female, her short white hair a startling contrast with her sun-blackened skin. She asks for his cloak to cover her shame and weakness—by which she means that she is female. Abba Macarius healed a little girl who was desperately ill, her flesh eaten away, full of worms and stench. He comforted her by saying that her illness was sent from God to save her from danger; and 'he restored her health, but in such a way that no femininity showed in her form, no female parts were apparent, so that in all her contact with men, she never beguiled them with womanly deceits' (Rufinus, *History* of the Monks of Egypt 28, PL 21. 451). The admirable Susan (Harvey 1990: 124–5) was the acknowledged leader of a double community of Monophysite monks and nuns. She had taken a vow always to veil her head and look downwards: she was afraid of the effect she might have on men, or they on her, if she looked them in the face.

5.3. *Philosophic Women*

In practice, the difference between a Christian and a non-Christian woman who wanted to lead a virtuous life was the option of renouncing marriage. Most traditions said that the philosopher Hypatia, daughter of a mathematician, refused to marry. One (wrong on dates) married her to the philosopher Isidore, who according to Damascius was by far her superior, 'not only as a man surpasses a woman, but as a real philosopher surpasses a geometrician' (fr. 164 Zintzen). There are no other examples of non-Christian women who opted for celibacy. The remarkable Sosipatra, according to Eunapius (*Lives* 469), was initiated in youth into the Chaldaean mysteries, and not only had effortless understanding of poetry, philosophy, and rhetoric but saw visions of the future and of events at a distance. This configuration of gifts is typical of the 'holy man' or holy woman (Fowden 1982). Sosipatra decided to marry at the appropriate age, informing her future husband that they would have three sons, who would not achieve worldly success. It was not her father's decision. He had abandoned any attempt to control his daughter's life, though he did sometimes wish she would say something: silence was also a characteristic of the profound philosopher.

There was no organization to support a non-Christian woman who did choose celibacy, unless she was that rare phenomenon, the virgin priestess of a cult (see above, Sect. 3.3). Moreover, a non-Christian woman would be unlikely to accept the Christian argument that there is no need for more human beings. Christian women, like Christian men, were asked to reflect that human society is deeply flawed and should not be perpetuated: far better to save, by prayer and renunciation, one's own soul and the souls of others already in existence, than to involve oneself in reproduction and the cares of the world. Theological argument emphasized undistracted commitment to God, freedom from anxiety about one's family and from sexual desire, and triumph over the downward drag of fallen human nature. Christians were told that human beings can, in this life, live like angels, reversing the fall of Adam and Eve into disobedience, desire, and death.

Besides the theological reasoning, there was a quite explicit argument about the distastefulness of married life, the demands of sexuality and child-bearing, and the subordination of women to their fathers, husbands, and family purposes generally. This is the aspect which has most impressed recent commentators, who find it hard to believe that renunciation and denial of sexuality could in themselves be a path to God. The majority of extant treatises on virginity are addressed to women. This may suggest that women had greater religious commitment, or were more eager than men to avoid marriage, but perhaps the reverse is true: women needed more convincing. A woman who did not marry renounced her only social role and might come under great family pressure. A man could opt to renounce marriage without renouncing a career: he could make compromises and had more freedom of choice. But it is only fair to say that, if the recurrent complaints about pseudo-virgins and merry widows are at all justified, some women did use the option of celibacy to avoid marriage and enjoy an active social life.[4]

Philosophic men had, since the fourth century BC, been told that the Wise Man would marry even if he would rather study and contemplate without the distractions of a household: he had an obligation to supply grandchildren for his parents, citizens for his homeland, and worshippers for the gods. So far as I know, no philosopher discussed the obligations of the would-be wise woman: her marriage was taken for granted. But a philosophic woman might hope to spend only a short

---

[4] On the motives for the choice of celibacy, see Brown (1988); Averil Cameron (1989, 1991); also, more briefly, Drijvers (1987); Bremmer (1989). Van Eijk (1972) emphasizes the triumph over mortality, Crouzel (1982) the single-minded commitment, Rousselle (1988) reluctance to marry. E. A. Clark (1983b) surveys Christian teaching on celibacy with special reference to John Chrysostom; Pagels (1988) is a more wide-ranging survey.

period of life in child-bearing, and could be encouraged to use her domestic life as a way of manifesting virtue. There was no need to think of herself as permanently trapped in femaleness.

'So do not worry whether you are male or female in body, and do not see yourself as a woman, for I did not draw near to you as such. Avoid all feminization of the soul, just as if you had a male body also. The most blessed offspring come from a virgin soul and a celibate mind.' Porphyry's words to his wife Marcella (*To Marcella* 33) are an extreme case in that she already had children and he had no wish for children—she was the widow of a friend and he had married her only to give her protection. Theosebius (Damascius, fr. 311 Zintzen) was probably more typical in offering his wife a 'ring of chastity', as he had formerly offered her a wedding-ring for living together and procreating children. But it is characteristic of the philosophic woman to be born into, and/or married into, a philosophic household, and to be taught that femaleness is no bar to philosophy provided she does not behave as untaught women do.

Marcella, according to Porphyry (*To Marcella* 3), is naturally suited to philosophy: she just needs the proper help, and her husband's friend is the person to give it. Within the same philosophic tradition, Plotinus had used the house of a wealthy widow for classes (Porphyry, *Life of Plotinus* 9); one of his students, Amphikleia, married the son of the 'divine' Iamblichus. Eunapius, writing the lives of philosophers, takes the opportunity to mention (*Lives* 477) his own cousin Melite, who married Iamblichus' pupil Chrysanthius. Iamblichus' circle included Arete; and in his *On the Pythagorean Life*, a work intended to inspire students of philosophy, Pythagorean women feature more than is to be expected in the context of Graeco-Roman philosophy (G. Clark 1989: pp. xvi–xviii). There are similar friendships and family connections among the Christian theologians of the late fourth century (Hunt 1982). The pattern continued: Damascius dedicated his *Life of Isidore the Philosopher* to Theodora (not the empress), who with her sisters had been taught both by Isidore and by Damascius, and whose interests extended beyond literature even to arithmetic and geometry. ('Even' because it was possible to absorb the ethical and religious teachings of philosophy without studying the mathematics which, as many philosophers believed, expressed or underlay the nature of the universe: O'Meara 1989.) Hypatia, daughter of Theon the mathematician, was both mathematician and philosopher.

It is not easy to discover what these philosophic women did, other than listen to discussions and manifest virtue (cf. Wicker 1987: 34–5). The wife of Maximus (according to Eunapius, who disapproved of him) made him look like a complete amateur in philosophy—but when they were summoned to the court of Julian she talked to the women who came in by the side door, while Maximus received all the leading men. All we know about the beliefs of this lady is that Eunapius (*Lives* 477) admired her, and this may have been for her piety and strong-mindedness rather than for her technical ability. Sosipatra is another matter. Eunapius (ibid. 466, 469) found that she deserved to be included in a work on the lives of great philosophers: he ranked her even above her brilliant husband' Eustathius, the only man worthy of her, making it clear that Sosipatra's soul (and she knew it) would be on a higher level after their deaths. Sosipatra did actually teach philosophy. As a widow she returned to Pergamum, where her friend the philosopher Aedesius educated her sons, and she was his rival in philosophy: she 'set up her chair' in her own house, and students would come to her after they had heard Aedesius' lecture. We find her (ibid. 469–70) delivering an inspired discourse on the soul, in a state of exaltation; but she has first demolished various arguments, so it is clear that she is not merely possessed, the ignorant vehicle of some greater force. Hypatia (Rist 1965: 216, 220) taught her own students, but was also a public figure in Alexandria, lecturing on Plato and Aristotle and moving freely through the streets dressed in her philosopher's cloak. Both the content and the fact of her teaching no doubt contributed to her being lynched by a Christian mob. The Arian writer Philostorgius disapproved of the lynching strongly enough to blame it on the rival faction of 'homoousian' Christians.

Nothing survives of what Sosipatra and Hypatia taught, unless perhaps we have some mathematical writing by Hypatia (Waithe 1987). This may be, in part, the effect of social convention. Most women did not write for general circulation or contribute to debate, and if they did there was a failure to take notice. Men did not usually correspond with women: it would not, as a rule, have been proper if the woman was not a close relative. Jerome's extensive correspondence with women may well have been a factor in his being asked to leave Rome. Besides, the major reasons for letter-writing were to display literary talent, make contacts, and request favours, and for this men really were more use. John Chrysostom's letters to Olympias are an exception, asking her to use her influence and to find things out for him, but her social status in Constantinople and his position as its exiled bishop were exceptional too.

When there was correspondence, men appear to have kept copies of their own letters, but not of the women's (Rousselle 1988: 179–83). In many centuries women who wrote no formal literary works have written brilliant letters, or kept diaries, or recorded their spiritual struggles. They may well have done so in late antiquity, but nothing survives. We do not have the elder Melania's letters to Evagrius (Jerome, *Letter* 133. 3, PL 22. 1151), or letters to Jerome from Paula, Eustochium, Demetrias, Hedybia, Marcella, Furia, and the others who con-. sulted him about exegesis and the Christian life. We do not know how Ambrose's elder sister Marcellina, a consecrated woman, responded to his accounts of power-struggles with the emperor, or what Augustine's sister thought of his instructions for the running of her convent. More than fifteen hundred letters of the orator Libanius, teacher of John Chrysostom, survive: four are addressed to women (Schouler 1985). The most interesting of these (*Letter* 677) is to Mariane, wife of the philosopher Sarpedon, and gives news of her friend Alexandra whose brother was a student with Libanius. It cannot be said to have philosophical content.

There is one possible example of philosophical work by a woman, but it is difficult to assess. Gregory of Nyssa professes to report (*On the Soul and Resurrection*, PG 46. 11–160) the arguments of his sister Macrina 'the teacher', on her death-bed, about the immortality and resurrection of the soul. Macrina, he declares elsewhere (*Life of Macrina* 3, PG 46. 961), had no formal training: her mother had educated her in the psalms and the Wisdom of Solomon, not in unsuitable classical culture. We may feel bound to allow for the conventions of the philosophical dialogue and for a Christian wish to demonstrate that prayer and meditation on Scripture was in itself a training in philosophy. (Thus Augustine's mother, Monica, who was untrained in philosophy and took no part in her son's debates with his friends, may bring a philosophical dialogue to an end by singing a hymn which is seen to give perfect expression to their conclusions on the Trinity: *On the Blessed Life* 35, PL 32. 976). On the other hand (Wolfskeel 1987), Macrina was one of an energetic and intelligent family, daughter of a very competent mother, and with brothers who had the university education that she was not offered.

Primary education, which was often coeducational, included some study of literature, if only as a way of teaching literacy (Kaster 1983). Girls and women who progressed further did so by private tuition and family support.[5] There is some evidence that the educated classes approved of educated women. For instance, a wedding-poem on the marriage of Maria, daughter of the great general Stilicho, to the heir apparent, makes the point that she was not thinking about marriage: she was happily reading Latin and Greek texts (Homer, Orpheus, and Sappho) with her mother (Claudian, poem 10. 229–37). This is clearly a credit to both of them. When Augustine interrogates himself on whether he has really given up worldly goods, the most tempting prospect is a wife: 'pretty, modest, obliging, educated or easily educable by you, bringing you just enough dowry—since you despise riches—to make her no kind of burden on your cultivated leisure, especially if you hope (indeed, you are sure) she would cause you no trouble' (*Soliloquies* 1. 10. 17, PL 32. 878). It was quite possible for women, given such support, to reach a high level of culture, but within limits. Many women were well read in both Latin and Greek, but they were expected to speak and write in a different style, and to have a different intellectual background, from that of an educated man. They were not trained in formal

---

[5] There is no entry for 'women' in the classic work on education in the ancient world, Marrou (1956): given the date, this is not surprising.

rhetorical skills, which included the manipulation of cultural references. Similarly, women writing in English from the seventeenth to the nineteenth century were often untrained in 'the classics', that is in Greek and Latin literature and the formal style derived from them. (The difference survives even in the 1950s novels of Angela Thirkell, daughter of a classical scholar, who much preferred 'educated' women—that is, those not formally educated but with a particular kind of general culture—to women who had been to college; but hers are consciously nostalgic works.) Christianity reinforced the traditional difference: it was just not practicable to educate a Christian boy without the grand old fortifying classical curriculum, but a Christian girl could be nurtured on Scripture and selected commentators. If Jerome is writing to women, he will quote Scripture and the Fathers rather than the classics—unless the letter is really for a wider public (E. A. Clark 1979: 72–6). It would have been bad manners—literary or conversational—to suppose that women cared for the formal style.

Sidonius describes the library of a senator's villa in southern France:

There were quantities of books ready to hand . . . so arranged that the books by the ladies' chairs were of a devotional [*religiosus*] style, and those by the gentlemen's benches were distinguished by the stateliness of Latin eloquence. But some of these, by certain authors, maintained the same level of style for a different purpose: men of comparable learning—Augustine and Varro, Horace and Prudentius—were constantly read. (*Letter* 2. 9. 4)

Sidonius' men friends do not lack religious commitment, provided they can nurture it in the style to which they are accustomed. His friend Hesperius (ibid. *Letter* 2. 10. 5) thought that one really cannot exercise rhetorical or poetical skill in the company of women. Sidonius encourages him with examples of wives who 'held the candlestick' while their husbands read and thought.

But women could do better than that. Athenais, renamed Eudocia, wife of Theodosius II, was educated by her father, an Athenian sophist. She could produce elegant verse: a tribute to the baths at Gadara has recently been discovered there (*JRS* 76. 144). When she delivered an address to the people of Antioch, she composed the praises of their city in hexameters; and she was capable of emending 'Homerocentones', rearrangements of Homer, in line with properly Homeric forms. This was not just a demonstration of technical skill: she was using her scholarship, as Proba did with her cento of Virgil, to integrate Christian and classical culture (Alan Cameron 1982: 270–89; E. A. Clark 1986: 124–71). She also wrote verse paraphrases of books of the Bible and hexameters on the deaths of martyrs. What is much more remarkable is that she could, apparently, deploy public rhetorical skills.

Eudocia was an exceptional woman in an exceptional position. Other women found their Christian commitment the best possible justification for study and debate. The serious study of the Bible could be intellectually demanding. For instance, Eustathius translated into Latin Basil's *Hexaemeron* 1–9 (reflections on the Six Days of Creation as described in Genesis), and dedicated it to his sister. It has to be admitted that the dedication of a learned work does not always prove that the dedicatee would like to read it, but there were women who would certainly have welcomed it. Paula and her daughters Blesilla and Eustochium studied Hebrew as well as exegesis. The younger Melania, according to her awestruck biographer, wrote—without mistakes—in notebooks; she read Scripture and homilies and (as a treat) the lives of the Fathers, and any other Christian writing she could lay her hands on; if she read in Greek it sounded like her native language (*Life of Melania* 23, 26). The elder Melania read 'millions' of lines of Origen (Palladius, *Lausiac History* 55). Caesaria the Patrician (Harvey 1990: 127) devoted years of study to her seven hundred volumes of the Fathers. A Bible commentary, in late antiquity, was very often a work of philosophy as well as learned exegesis, and these women who did not write their own commentaries showed their ability in reading them. It is not enough to dismiss them with the assertion that 'Christian women leaders had to know the Bible, and perhaps had to know how to sing in tune' (Momigliano 1987: 346).

It would be pleasant, but unrealistic, to end on this high

note. The women whom we know to have engaged in such
study were of exceptional social status. They may have served
as role-models, but their achievements did not necessarily
make life any different for girls growing up. The potential for
change was there, but it was not developed. The women's communities for which Augustine and, following him, Caesarius
wrote rules were expected to have a sister in charge of books as
well as one in charge of woolwork. Caesarius was committed
to literacy as a means of understanding Scripture: he required
nuns to learn letters if necessary, and to read for two hours
every day. When his own sister Caesaria was abbess (Caesarius,
Life 1. 58), she required the nuns to make fine copies of
religious books: this may even mean (Chadwick 1990: 39)
illuminated manuscripts, but probably what she wanted was
clear and legible copies for distribution. This concern for
education stops short before taking girls into convents just to
be taught. Basil (*Longer Rules* 15, PG 31. 952) envisaged taking
children into the communities for which he made regulations,
but Caesarius (*Rule* 5) said it should not be done: perhaps they
would have been too distracting, or too vivid a reminder of the
other possibilities of life.

CONCLUSION

THERE cannot be a conclusion to a patchwork: only edges when it seems big enough for the purpose. Every scrap of material should come labelled with date and place of origin, purpose and prejudices, social level. Some pieces should not be sewn together with others. We can sometimes see fragments of a pattern, but no overall design. It would (for instance) be possible to give an optimistic account of women's rights and status in late antiquity, one which is quite impressive by the standards of the Graeco-Roman world if not by those of the late-twentieth-century West. We could argue that post-classical law shows a general tendency, made explicit in Justinian's legislation, to respect women's control over their property and their own bodies. Medical theory supported this by treating women as physically similar to men; doctors and midwives influenced by Soranus would be unlikely to see marriage and pregnancy as a cure for most female problems. Both Christian and non-Christian philosophy encouraged women to think of themselves as capable of goodness, and it was possible for them, even in their domestic setting, to reach a very high level of literary and philosophical culture. But we cannot generalize. We do not know how far Justinian's codification of law differed from previous law; we do know (from Egyptian papyri) that imperial legislation and law 'on the ground' did not coincide, and (from the law codes themselves) that many people's lives were in practice unaffected. Medical theories varied, and it is not clear how many people they influenced; and the ideology of femaleness had different aspects, so that strength or weakness could be invoked according to need.

The texture overall, I think, is that of inherited assumptions. We continue to be told, as at any time since the fifth century BC, that women are domestic, and that what they actually do with their time is not very interesting. Public status is inappropriate for them unless they are members of the imperial house, and even then they are expected to manifest the traditional virtues of modesty, chastity, and piety towards gods and family. Women's purpose in life is marriage and child-bearing, and this is also the most important factor in their health. They must be protected from exploitation of their weakness by untrustworthy men and prevented from immodest self-assertion against trustworthy ones. Their characteristic faults are talking too much and concern for their appearance, and they need help to keep their impulses in check. There are good women, who are faithful, modest, and competent in their domestic lives, and are able to understand and act upon moral principles; but, although they are just as capable as men of being good, they will normally manifest their goodness in private life.

Some of these inherited assumptions were challenged by Christian beliefs, but it is misleading to ask whether Christianity, as such, made people think differently about women or treat them better. Christian teaching could either reinforce or subvert traditional beliefs about women—and it could use the traditional beliefs to construct Christian teaching. It could devalue even the faithful and fertile wife by suggesting that her concerns were a mixture of lust, squalor, and irrelevance, or it could insist that women must tailor their asceticism to the wishes of fathers and husbands. Women could be pressured into celibacy as they could be pressured into marriage. The Christian claim that men and women are spiritually equal had no more practical consequences than the philosophical claim that women can manifest the same virtues as men.

But Christianity did enlarge the possibilities for women. The really important shift of belief here is that commitment to God may require, in both men and women, abandonment of duties to family and State. For the first time, women (some women) could reject marriage and child-bearing, and live at home with their mothers, or in solitude, or in a community of women. Prayer and Bible study could displace domestic life, whereas literature and philosophy had had to fit round it. Women had always been able to take part in religious cult and make offerings to the gods, but they could now achieve lasting fame by devoting their wealth to the Church and themselves to

God's service. Spiritual struggles became as interesting as politics: women still hardly ever wrote books, but people wrote books about women.

We may well be shocked by the general Christian disparagement of femaleness, the sufferings some women inflicted on themselves and their families, and the praise which their behaviour evoked. (There are parallels with the efforts of women in the 1960s and 1970s to escape from the feminine role.) We cannot pronounce on the spiritual gains or losses. But there were some practical gains, not just for those who became famous, but for the women of the poor whose lives at last come into focus. A member of Melania's community once asked her (*Life of Melania* 62) how she withstood spiritual pride in her own asceticism. If she were tempted, she replied, she would think of people who were starving rather than fasting, or prisoners, or desperately poor, or sleeping rough in the cold. Some such women, at least, were acknowledged as members of the Church, given food and clothing from the benefactions of rich people on whom they had no personal claim, rescued from dying in the streets, or even taken into women's communities whose austerity was greater comfort than they had ever known. I shall end with them.

REFERENCES

Adnès, A., and Canivet, P. (1967), 'Guérisons miraculeuses et exorcisme dans l'*Histoire Philothée* de Théodoret de Cyr', *Revue de l'Histoire des Religions*, 171: 53–82, 149–79.

Amunsden, D. W., and Diers, C. J. (1969), 'The Age of Menarche in Classical Greece and Rome', *Human Biology*, 41: 125–32.

———— (1970), 'The Age of Menopause in Classical Greece and Rome', *Human Biology*, 42: 79–86.

André J. (1981), *L'Alimentation et la cuisine à Rome* (Paris: Les Belles Lettres).

Anson, J. (1974), 'The Female Transvestite in Early Monasticism: The Origin and Development of a Motif', *Viator*, 5: 1–32.

Arjava, A. (1988), 'Divorce in Later Roman Law', *Arctos*, 22: 5–21.

—— (forthcoming), *Women and Law in Late Antiquity.*

Bagnall, R. S. (1987), 'Church, State and Divorce in Late Roman Egypt', in K.-L. Selig and R. Somerville (eds.), *Florilegium Columbianum: Essays in Honour of Paul Oskar Kristeller* (New York: Italica Press), 41–61.

Barber, C. (1990), 'The Imperial Panels at San Vitale: A Reconsideration', *Byzantine and Modern Greek Studies*, 14: 19–42.

Beaucamp, J. (1976), 'Le Vocabulaire de la faiblesse féminine dans les textes juridiques romains du 3e au 6e siècle', *Revue de l'histoire du droit français et étranger*, 4: 485–508.

—— (1977), 'La Situation juridique de la femme à Byzance', *Cahiers de civilisation mediévale*, 20: 145–76.

—— (1985), 'Le Veuvage dans les papyrus byzantins', *Pallas* 32: 149–57.

—— (1990), *Le Statut de la femme à Byzance (4e-7e siècle)*, i. *Le droit impérial* (Paris: Boccard).

Berrouard, M. F., O. P. (1972), 'Saint Augustin et l'indissolubilité du mariage: L'Évolution de sa pensée', *Studia Patristica*, 11 (= *Texte und Untersuchungen* 108): 291–306.

Birks, P., and McLeod, G. (1987), *Justinian's Institutes* (London: Duckworth).

Blayney, J. (1986), 'Theories of Conception in the Ancient Roman world', in B. Rawson (ed.), *The Family in Ancient Rome* (London: Croom Helm), 230–6.

Boswell, J. (1980), *Christianity, Social Tolerance and Homosexuality:*

Gay People in Western Europe from the Beginning of the Christian Era to the Fourteenth Century (Chicago: University of Chicago Press).

——(1989), *The Kindness of Strangers: The Abandonment of Children in Western Europe from Late Antiquity to the Renaissance* (New York: Random House).

Bowersock, G. (1990), *Hellenism in Late Antiquity* (Cambridge: Cambridge University Press).

Boylan, M. (1984), 'The Galenic and Hippocratic Challenges to Aristotle's Conception Theory', *Journal of the History of Biology*, 17: 83–112.

Bradley, K. (1991), *Discovering the Roman Family: Studies in Roman Social History* (Oxford: Oxford University Press).

Bremmer, J. (1989), 'Why did early Christianity attract upper-class women?', in A. A. R. Bastiaensen *et al.* (eds.), *Fructus Centesimus: Mélanges offerts à Gérard J. M. Bartelink* (Steenbrugge, in Abbatia S. Petri), 117–34.

Brock, S., and Harvey, S. A. (1987), *Holy Women of the Syrian Orient* (Berkeley, Calif.: University of California Press).

Brown, P. (1981), *The Cult of the Saints: Its Rise and Function in Latin Christianity* (London: SCM).

——(1987), 'Late Antiquity', in P. Veyne (ed.), *A History of Private Life, i. From Pagan Rome to Byzantium* (Cambridge: Mass.: Belknap).

——(1988), *The Body and Society: Men, Women and Sexual Renunciation in Early Christianity* (New York: Columbia University Press).

Buckland, W. W. (1975), *A Textbook of Roman Law from Augustus to Justinian*, ed. P. G. Stein (3rd edn., Cambridge: Cambridge University Press).

Bullough, V. L. (1985), 'Merchandising the Sanitary Napkin: Lillian Gilbreth's 1927 Survey', *Signs*, 10: 615–27.

Cameron, Alan (1982), 'The Empress and the Poet', *Yale Classical Studies*, 27: 217–89.

Cameron, Averil (1978), 'The Cult of the Theotokos in Sixth-Century Constantinople', *Journal of Theological Studies*, NS 29: 79–108.

——(1979a), 'The Virgin's Robe: An Episode in the History of Seventh-Century Constantinople', *Byzantion*, 49: 42–56.

——(1979b), review of Honoré 1978, *Journal of Roman Studies*, 79: 199–201.

——(1985), *Procopius and the Sixth Century* (London: Duckworth).

—— (1986), *Procopius* (London: Duckworth).

—— (1989), 'Virginity as Metaphor', in A. Cameron (ed.), *History as Text* (London: Duckworth), 181–205.

—— (1991), *Christianity and the Rhetoric of Empire* (Berkeley, Calif.: University of California Press).

Chadwick, H. (1979), 'The Relativity of Moral Codes: Rome and Persia in Late Antiquity', in W. R. Schoedel and R. L. Wilken (eds.), *Early Christian Literature and the Classical Tradition: In honorem R. M. Grant* (Paris: Beauchesne), 135–53.

Chadwick, W. (1990), *Women, Art and Society* (London: Thames and Hudson).

Clark, E. A. (1979), *Jerome, Chrysostom and Friends* (New York: Edwin Mellen).

—— (1983*a*), *Women in the Early Church* (Wilmington, Del.: Michael Glazier).

—— (1983*b*), Introduction, in *John Chrysostom: On Virginity, Against Remarriage*, trans. S. R. Shore (Studies in Women and Religion, 9; Lewiston, NY: Edwin Mellen Press).

—— (1984), *The Life of Melania the Younger* (New York: Edwin Mellen).

—— (1986), *Ascetic Piety and Women's Faith* (New York: Edwin Mellen).

Clark, G. (1989), *Iamblichus: On the Pythagorean Life* (Translated Texts for Historians; Liverpool: Liverpool University Press).

Cohen, S. J. D. (1991), 'Menstruants and the Sacred', in S. B. Pomeroy (ed.), *Women's History and Ancient History* (Chapel Hill, NC: University of North Carolina Press), 273–99.

Corbett, P. E. (1930), *The Roman Law of Marriage* (Oxford: Oxford University Press).

Corbier, M. (1990), 'Les Comportements familiaux de l'aristocratie romaine (du deuxième siècle avant Jésus-Christ au troisième siècle après Jésus-Christ)', in J. Andreau and H. Bruhns (eds.), *Parenté et stratégies familiales dans l'antiquité romaine* (Collections de l'École Française de Rome, 129; Rome: École Française de Rome).

Crawford, P. (1981), 'Attitudes to Menstruation in Seventeenth-Century England', *Past and Present*, 91: 45–73.

Crook, J. (1986), 'Feminine Inadequacy and the SC Velleianum', in B. Rawson (ed.), *The Family in Ancient Rome* (London: Croom Helm).

Crouzel, H. (1971), *L'Église primitive face au divorce du premier au cinquième siècle* (Théologie Historique, 13; Paris: Beauchesne).

—— (1982), *Mariage et divorce, célibat et caractère sacerdotaux dans l'église ancienne* (Turin: Bottega d'Erasmo).

Culham, P. (1982), 'The Lex Oppia', *Latomus*, 41: 786–93.

—— (1986), 'Again, what meaning lies in Colour!', *Zeitschrift für Papyrologie und Epigraphik*, 64: 235–45.

de Mendieta, D. A., and Moons, M. C. (1953) 'Une curieuse homélie grecque inédite sur la virginité adressée aux pères de famille', *Revue Bénédictine*, 63: 18–69, 211–38.

Dean-Jones, L. (1989), 'Menstrual Bleeding according to the Hippocratics and Aristotle', *Transactions of the American Philological Association*, 119: 179–94.

Dixon, S. (1984), 'Infirmitas sexus: Womanly Weakness in Roman Law', *Tijdschrift voor Rechtsgeschiedenis*, 52: 343–71.

—— (1988), *The Roman Mother* (London: Croom Helm).

Drijvers, J. (1987), 'Virginity and Asceticism in Late Roman Western Élites', in J. Blok and P. Mason (eds.) *Sexual Asymmetry* (Amsterdam: Gieben), 241–73.

Duffy, J. (1984), 'Byzantine Medicine in the Sixth and Seventh Centuries: Aspects of Teaching and Practice', *Dumbarton Oaks Papers*, 34: 21–7.

Dunstan, G. R. (1990) (ed.), *The Human Embryo: Aristotle and the Arabic and European traditions* (Exeter: Exeter University Press).

Edelstein, L. (1967), *Ancient Medicine: Selected Papers of Ludwig Edelstein*, trans. O. Temkin (Baltimore: Johns Hopkins).

Ellis, S. (1985), 'The Palace of the Dux at Apollonia, and Related Examples', in G. Barker, J. Lloyd, and J. Reynolds (eds.), *Cyrenaica in Antiquity* (British Archaeological Reports, International Series, 236; Oxford: BAR), 15–25.

—— (1991), 'Power, Architecture and Decor: How the Late Roman Aristocrat Appealed to his Guests', in E. K. Gazda (ed.) *Roman Art in the Private Sphere* (Ann Arbor, Mich.: University of Michigan Press).

Elm, S. K. (1987), 'The Organization and Institutions of Female Asceticism in Fourth-Century Cappadocia and Egypt', Oxford D. Phil. thesis.

—— (1991), 'Evagrius Ponticus' *Sententiae ad Virginem*', *Dumbarton Oaks Papers*, 45: 97–120.

Emmett, A. M. (1984), 'An Early Fourth-Century Female Monastic Community in Egypt?', in A. Moffatt (ed.), *Maistor: Classical, Byzantine and Renaissance Studies for Robert Browning* (Canberra: Byzantina Australiensia).

Étienne, R. (1973), 'La Conscience médicale antique et la vie des enfants', *Annales de démographie historique*, 9: 15–61.

Evans-Grubbs, J. (1987), 'Munita Coniugia: The Emperor

Constantine's Legislation on Marriage and the Family' (Ph.D. Stanford University: UMI dissertations).

—— (1989), 'Abduction Marriage in Antiquity: A Law of Constantine (CTh IX. 24. 1) and its Social Context', *Journal of Roman Studies*, 79: 59–83.

Fisher, E. A. (1978), 'Theodora and Antonina in the *Historia Arcana*: History and/or Fiction?', *Arethusa*, 11: 253–79.

Floeri, F. (1953), 'Le Sens de la division des sexes chez Grégoire de Nysse', *Revue de sciences religieuses*, 27: 105–11.

Fowden, G. (1982), 'The Pagan Holy Man in Late Antique Society', *Journal of Hellenic Studies*, 102: 33–59.

Frier, B. (1982), 'Roman Life Expectancy: Ulpian's Evidence', *Harvard Studies in Classical Philology*, 86: 213–51.

Gardner, J. (1986), *Women in Roman Law and Society* (London: Croom Helm).

Geddes, A. G. (1987), 'Rags and Riches: The Costume of Athenian Men in the Fifth Century, *Classical Quarterly*, 37: 307–31.

Goody, J. (1983), *The Development of the Family and Marriage in Europe* (Cambridge: Cambridge University Press).

Gould, G. (1990), 'Women in the Writings of the Fathers: Language, Belief and Reality', in W. J. Sheils and D. Wood (eds.) *Women and the Church* (Studies in Church History, 27; Oxford: Blackwell), 1–13.

Graef, H. (1966), 'The Theme of the Second Eve in Some Byzantine Sermons on the Assumption', *Studia patristica* 9 (Texte und Untersuchungen, 94; Berlin), 224–30.

Granger-Taylor, H. (1982), 'Weaving Clothes to Shape in the Ancient World', *Textile History*, 13: 3–10.

—— (forthcoming), *Purple and Gold: Textiles and Clothing of Classical Antiquity* (Philadelphia: Yale University Press).

Grmek, M. D. (1988), *Diseases in the Ancient Greek World* (ET; Baltimore: Johns Hopkins).

Hanson, A. E. (1987), 'The Eight-Months Child and the Etiquette of birth: Obsit omen!', *Bulletin of the History of Medicine*, 61: 589–602.

—— (1989), review of Jackson 1988, *Journal of Roman Archaeology*, 2: 299–304.

—— (1990), 'The Medical Writers' Woman', in D. Halperin, J. J. Winkler, and F. Zeitlin (eds.), *Before Sexuality: The Construction of Erotic Experience in the Greek World* (Princeton, NJ: Princeton University Press), 309–38.

Harries, J. (1984), 'Treasures in Heaven: Property and Inheritance among Senators of Late Rome', in E. M. Craik (ed.), *Marriage and Property* (Aberdeen: Aberdeen University Press).

—— (1988), 'The Roman Imperial Quaestor from Constantine to Theodosius II', *Journal of Roman Studies*, 78: 148–72.

—— and Wood, I. (forthcoming), *Theodosian Code* (London: Duckworth).

Harrison, M. (1989), *A Temple for Byzantium: The Discovery and Excavation of Anicia Juliana's Palace Church in Istanbul* (London: Harvey Miller).

Harvey, S. A. (1990), *Asceticism and Society in Crisis: John of Ephesus and the Lives of the Eastern Saints* (Berkeley, Calif.: University of California Press).

Herrin, J. (1983), 'In Search of Byzantine Women', in A. Cameron and A. Kuhrt (eds.), *Images of Women in Antiquity* (London: Routledge), 167–89.

Holdsworth, A. (1988), *Out of the Dolls House: the Story of Women in the Twentieth Century* (London: BBC).

Hollander, A. (1975), *Seeing through Clothes* (New York: Viking Press).

Holum, K. (1982), *Theodosian Empresses: Women and Imperial Dominion in Late Antiquity* (Berkeley, Calif.: University of California Press).

Honoré, T. (1978), *Tribonian* (London: Duckworth).

—— (1981), *Emperors and Lawyers* (London: Duckworth).

—— (1982), *Ulpian* (Oxford: Oxford University Press).

Hopkins, K. (1965*a*), 'Contraception in the Roman Empire', *Comparative Studies in Society and History*, 8 (1965–6): 124–51.

—— (1965*b*), 'The Age of Roman Girls at Marriage', *Population Studies*, 18: 309–27.

Horden, P. (1982), 'Saints and Doctors in Early Byzantine History: The Case of Theodore of Sykeon', in W. J. Sheils (ed.) *The Church and Healing* (Studies in Church History, 19: Oxford: Blackwell), 1–13.

Horowitz, M. C. (1979), 'The Image of God in Man—is Woman included?', *Harvard Theological Review*, 72: 175–206.

Houston, M. G. (1947), *Ancient Greek, Roman and Byzantine Costume* (London: Black).

Huchthausen, L. (1974), 'Herkunft und ökonomische Stellung weiblicher Adressaten von Reskripten des *Codex Iustinianus* (2. und 3. Jh.u.Z.)', *Klio*, 56: 199–228.

—— (1976), 'Zu kaiserlichen Reskripten an weibliche Adressaten aus der Zeit Diokletians (284–305 u.Z.)', *Klio*, 58: 55–85.

Humbert, M. (1972), *Le Remariage à Rome: Étude d'histoire juridique et sociale* (Milan: Giuffré).

Hunt, E. D. (1982), *Holy Land Pilgrimage in the Later Roman Empire AD 312–460* (Oxford: Oxford University Press).

Hunter, D. G. (1987), 'Resistance to the Virginal Ideal in Late Fourth Century Rome: The Case of Jovinian', *Theological Studies*, 48: 45–64.

—— (1989), '*On the Sin of Adam and Eve*: A Little Known Defense of Marriage and Childbearing by Ambrosiaster', *Harvard Theological Review*, 82: 283–99.

Jackson, R. (1988), *Doctors and Diseases in the Roman Empire* (London: British Museum Publications).

—— (1990), 'Roman Doctors and their Instruments: Modern Research into Ancient Problems', *Journal of Roman Archaeology*, 3: 5–27.

Jacquart, D., and Thomasset, C. (1988), *Sexuality and Medicine in the Middle Ages* (ET; London: Polity Press).

Jolowicz, H., and Nicholas, B. (1972), *A Historical Introduction to Roman Law* (3rd edn.; Cambridge: Cambridge University Press).

Jones, A. H. M. (1964), *The Later Roman Empire 284–602*, 2 vols. (Oxford: Blackwell).

Jones, H. (1988), 'Justiniani Novellae: Ou l'autoportrait d'un législateur', *Revue internationale des droits de l'antiquité*, 35: 149–208.

Kaster, R. A. (1983), 'Notes on Primary and Secondary Schools in Late Antiquity', *Transactions of the American Philological Association*, 113: 323–46.

Katzoff, R. (1985), '*Donatio ante nuptias* and Jewish Dowry Additions', *Yale Classical Studies*, 28: 231–44.

Kazhdan, A. (1990), 'Byzantine Hagiography and Sex in the Fifth to Twelfth Centuries', *Dumbarton Oaks Papers*, 44: 131–43.

King, H. (1983), 'Bound to Bleed', in A. Cameron and A. Kuhrt (eds.), *Images of Women in Antiquity* (London: Croom Helm), 109–27.

—— (1985), 'From Parthenos to Gynê: The Dynamics of Category', Ph.D. thesis (University College, London).

—— (1987), 'Sacrificial Blood: The Role of the *amnion* in Ancient Gynaecology', in M. B. Skinner (ed.), *Rescuing Creusa* (*Helios*, special issue 13/2): 117–26.

—— (1988), 'The Early Anodynes: Pain in the Ancient World', in R. D. Mann (ed.), *The History of the Management of Pain* (Park Ridge, NJ: Parthenon), 51–62.

—— (1989), 'The Daughter of Leonides: Reading the Hippocratic Corpus', in A. Cameron (ed.), *History as Text* (London: Duckworth), 13–32.

—— (1991), 'Using the Past: Nursing and the Medical Profession in Ancient Greece', in P. Holden and J. Littlewood (eds.), *Anthropology and Nursing* (London: Routledge), 7–24.

Kraemer, R. (1980), 'The Conversion of Women to Ascetic Forms of Christianity', *Signs*, 6: 298–307.

LaFontaine, J. (1970), 'La Femme dans la poésie de Prudence', *Revue des études latines*, 47bis (Mélanges M. Durry): 55–83.

Laistner, M. L. W. (1951), *Christianity and Pagan Culture in the Later Roman Empire*, together with an English translation of John Chrysostom's *Address on Vainglory* and *The Right Way for Parents to Bring Up their Children* (Ithaca, NY: Cornell University Press).

Laqueur, T. G. (1990), *Making Sex: Body and Gender from the Greeks to Freud* (Cambridge, Mass.: Harvard University Press).

Lardinois, A. (1989), 'Lesbian Sappho and Sappho of Lesbos', in J. Bremmer (ed.), *From Sappho to de Sade: Moments in the History of Sexuality* (London: Routledge), 15–35.

Lawless, G., OSA (1987), *Augustine of Hippo and his Monastic Rule* (Oxford: Oxford University Press).

Lee, A. D. (1988), 'Close-Kin Marriage in Late Antique Mesopotamia', *Greek Roman and Byzantine Studies*, 29: 403–13.

Lightman, M., and Zeisel, W. (1977), '*Univira*: An Example of Continuity and Change in Roman Society', *Church History*, 77: 19–32.

Longfield Jones, G. (1986), 'A Graeco-Roman Speculum in the Wellcome Museum', *Medical History*, 30: 81–9.

L'Orange, H. P. (1973), *Likeness and Icon: Selected Studies in Classical and Early Mediaeval Art* (Odense: Odense University Press).

Lurie, A. (1981), *The Language of Clothes* (London: Heinemann).

Maas, M. (1986), 'History and Ideology in Justinianic Reform Legislation', *Dumbarton Oaks Papers*, 40: 17–31.

MacCormack, S. (1981), *Art and Ceremony in Late Antiquity* (Berkeley, Calif.: University of California Press).

Macdonald, W. (1986), *The Architecture of the Roman Empire II: An Urban Appraisal* (New Haven, Conn.: Yale University Press).

McHugh, M. (1976), 'Linen, Wool and Colour: Their Appearance in St. Ambrose', *Bulletin of the Institute of Classical Studies*, 23: 99–101.

McLaren, A. (1990), *A History of Contraception from Antiquity to the Present Day* (Oxford: Blackwell).

MacMullen, R. (1964), 'Social Mobility and the Theodosian Code', *Journal of Roman Studies*, 54: 49–53.

——(1980), 'Women in Public in the Roman Empire', *Historia*, 29: 208–18.

——(1986a), 'What difference did Christianity make?', *Historia* 35: 322–43.

——(1986b), 'Judicial Savagery in the Roman Empire', *Chiron*, 16: 147–66.

——(1989), 'The Preacher's Audience (AD 350–400)', *Journal of Theological Studies*, 40: 503–11.

Macrides, R. (1990), 'Nomos and kanon on Paper and in Court', in R. Morris (ed.), *Church and People in Byzantium* (Birmingham: University of Birmingham).

Maguire, H. (1990), 'Garments Pleasing to God: The Significance of Domestic Textile Designs in the Early Byzantine Period', *Dumbarton Oaks Papers*, 44: 215–24.

Manfredini, A. (1988), 'Certi legum conditores et la veuve vierge (CI 1. 1. 5)', *Revue internationale des droits de l'antiquité*, 35: 209–22.

Mann, J. C. (1985), 'Epigraphic Consciousness', *Journal of Roman Studies*, 75: 204–6.

Marrou, H.-I. (1956), *A History of Education in Antiquity* (ET; London: Sheed and Ward).

Matthews, J. (1971), 'Gallic Supporters of Theodosius', *Latomus*, 30: 1083–7.

Meyendorff, J. (1990), 'Christian Marriage in Byzantium: The Canonical and Liturgical Tradition', *Dumbarton Oaks Papers*, 44: 99–107.

Millar, F. (1984), 'Condemnation to Hard Labour in the Roman Empire', *Papers of the British School at Rome*, NS 39: 124–47.

——(1986), 'A new approach to the Roman jurists', *Journal of Roman Studies*, 76: 272–80.

Miller, T. S. (1985), *The Birth of the Hospital in the Byzantine Empire* (Baltimore: Johns Hopkins).

Mills, H. (1984), 'Greek Clothing Regulations, Sacred and Profane', *Zeitschrift für Papyrologie und Epigraphik*, 55: 255–65.

Modrzejewski, J. (1970), 'La Règle de droit dans l'Egypte romaine', *American Studies in Papyrology*, 7 (ed. D. Samuel): 317–77.

Momigliano, A. (1987), 'The Life of St. Macrina by Gregory of Nyssa', in *Ottavo contributo alla storia degli studi classici e del mondo antico* (Storia e Letteratura; Rome, 1987), 333–47.

Mommsen, Th., and Meyer, P. (1954), *Theodosiani libri XVI* (2nd edn.; 3 vols.; Berlin: Weidmann).

Monnas, L., and Granger-Taylor, H. (1989) (eds.), *Ancient and Mediaeval Textiles: Studies in Honour of Donald King* (*Textile History*, 20; Pasold research fund).

Musurillo, H. (1956), 'The Problem of Ascetical Fasting in the Greek Patristic Fathers', *Traditio*, 12: 1–64.

Muthesius, A. (1989), 'From Seed to Samite: Aspects of Byzantine Silk Production', in Monnas and Granger-Taylor 1989: 135–49.

Noonan, J. T., jun. (1966), *Contraception: A History of its Treatment by the Catholic Theologians and Canonists* (Cambridge, Mass.: Belknap).

—— (1970) (ed.), *The Morality of Abortion: Legal and Historical Perspectives* (Cambridge, Mass.: Belknap).

Nürnberg, R. (1988), 'Non decet neque necessarium est, ut mulieres doceant', *Jahrbuch für Antike und Christentum*, 31: 51–73.

Nutton, V. (1977), '*Archiatri* and the Medical Profession in Antiquity', *Papers of the British School at Rome*, 45: 191–226.

—— (1984), 'From Galen to Alexander: Aspects of Medicine and Medical Practice in Late Antiquity', *Dumbarton Oaks Papers*, 38: 1–14.

—— (1986), Essay review of Miller 1985, *Medical History*, 30: 218–21.

—— (1988), *From Democedes to Harvey* (London: Variorum Reprints).

Oikonomides, N. (1976), 'Leo VI's Legislation Forbidding Fourth Marriages', *Dumbarton Oaks Papers*, 30: 173–93.

—— (1990), 'The Contents of the Byzantine House from the Eleventh to the Fifteenth Centuries', *Dumbarton Oaks Papers*, 44: 205–14.

O'Meara, D. J. (1989), *Pythagoras Revived: Mathematics and Philosophy in Late Antiquity* (Oxford: Oxford University Press).

Onians, J. (1980), 'Abstraction and Imagination in Late Antiquity', *Art History*, 3: 1–23.

Pagels, E. (1988), *Adam, Eve and the Serpent* (London: Weidenfeld and Nicholson).

Parker, R. (1983), *Miasma: Pollution and Purification in Early Greek Religion* (Oxford: Oxford University Press).

Patlagean, E. (1977), *Pauvreté économique et pauvreté sociale à Byzance, 4e–7e siècles* (Paris: Mouton).

—— (1981), *Structure sociale, famille, chrétienté à Byzance IVe–XIe siècle* (London: Variorum Reprints).

—— (1983), 'Ancient Byzantine Hagiography and Social History', in S. Wilson (ed.), *Saints and their Cults* (Cambridge: Cambridge University Press).

Payer, P. J. (1984), *Sex and the Penitentials: The Development of a Sexual Code 550–1150* (Toronto: University of Toronto Press).

Perrin, M. (1981), *L'Homme antique et chrétien: L'Anthropologie de Lactance* (Paris: Beauchesne).

Reinhold, M. (1970), *The History of Purple as a Status Symbol in Antiquity* (Collection Latomus, 116; Brussels: Latomus).

Riddle, J. M. (1981), 'Pseudo-Dioscorides *Ex herbis femininis* and Early Mediaeval Medical Botany', *Journal of the History of Biology*, 14: 43–81.

—— (1985), *Dioscorides on Pharmacy and Medicine* (Austin, Tex.: University of Texas Press).

—— (1991), 'Oral Contraceptives and Short-Term Abortifacients during Classical Antiquity and the Middle Ages', *Past and Present*, 132: 3–32.

Rist, J. M. (1965), 'Hypatia', *Phoenix*, 19: 214–25.

Roberts, M. (1990), *The Jewelled Style: Poetry and Poetics in Late Antiquity* (Ithaca, NY: Cornell University Press).

Robinson, O. (1987*a*), 'The Status of Women in Roman Private Law', *Juridical Review*, 2: 143–62.

—— (1987*b*), 'The Historical Background', in Sheila McLean and Noreen Burrows (eds.), *The Legal Relevance of Gender* (London: Macmillan).

Rossiter, J. J. (1989), 'Roman Villas in the Greek East and the Villa in Gregory of Nyssa *Ep.* 20', *Journal of Roman Archaeology*, 2: 101–10.

—— (1991), '*Convivium* and Villa in Late Antiquity', in W. J. Slater (ed.) *Dining in a Classical Context* (Ann Arbor, Mich.: University of Michigan Press), 119–214.

Rouche, M. (1987), 'The Early Middle Ages in the West', in P. Veyne (ed.), *A History of Private Life, i. From Pagan Rome to Byzantium* (Cambridge, Mass.: Belknap).

Rousselle, A. (1988), *Porneia: On Desire and the Body in Antiquity* (ET; Oxford: Blackwell).

—— (1991), 'La Politique des corps', in G. Duby and M. Perrot (eds.), *Histoire des femmes, i. L'Antiquité* (Paris: Plon), 319–59.

Russell, N. (1980), *The Lives of the Desert Fathers* (Oxford and London: Mowbray).

Saller, R. (1984), 'Roman Dowry and the Devolution of Property in the Principate', *Classical Quarterly*, 34: 195–205.

Salzmann, M. R. (1989), 'Aristocratic Women: Conductors of Christianity in the Fourth Century', *Helios*, 16/2: 207–20.

Schanzer, D. (1985), 'Merely a Cynic Gesture?', *Rivista di filologia*, 113: 61–6.

Scheltema, H. J. (1967), 'Byzantine Law', in J. M. Hussey (ed.), *The Byzantine Empire*, pt. II. *Government, Church and Civilization* (Cambridge Mediaeval History, iv; Cambridge University Press), 55–77.

Schouler, B. (1985), 'Libanios et les femmes de son temps', *Pallas*, 32: 123–48.

Schwarz, W. (1973), 'A Study in Pre-Christian Symbolism: Philo *de somniis* 1. 216–18, Plutarch *de Iside et Osiride* 4. 77', *Bulletin of the Institute of Classical Studies*, 23: 99–101.

Scobie, A. (1986), 'Slums, Sanitation and Mortality in the Roman World', *Klio*, 68: 399–433.

Secombe, W. (1990), 'Starting to Stop: Working-Class Fertility Decline in Britain', *Past and Present*, 126: 151–88.

Shaw, B. (1984), 'Latin Funerary Epigraphy and Family Life in the Later Roman Empire', *Historia*, 33: 457–97.

—— (1987), 'The Family in Late Antiquity: The Experience of Augustine', *Past and Present*, 115: 3–51.

——— and Saller. R. (1984), 'Close-Kin Marriage in Roman Society', *Man*, 19: 432–44.

Shore, S. R. (1983) (trans.), *John Chrysostom: On Virginity and Against. Remarriage* (Studies in Women and Religion, 9; Lewiston, NY: Edwin Mellen Press).

Singer, C. (1927), 'The Herbal in Antiquity and its Transmission to Later Ages', *Journal of Hellenic Studies*, 47: 1–52.

Sissa, G. (1990), *Greek Virginity* (ET; Cambridge, Mass.: Harvard University Press).

—— (1991), 'Philosophies du genre', in G. Duby and M. Perrot (eds.), *Histoire des femmes, i. L'Antiquité* (Paris: Plon), 65–99.

Smith, R. R. (1985), 'Roman Portraits: Honours, Empresses and Late Emperors', *Journal of Roman Studies*, 75: 209–21.

Sodini, J.-P., and Tate, G. (1984), 'Maisons d'époque romaine et byzantine (IIe–VIe siècles) du massif calcaire de Syrie du Nord: Étude typologique', in *Actes du Colloque Apamée de Syrie* (Paris: de Boccard).

Stein, P. G. (1988), 'Roman Law', in J. H. Burns (ed.), *Cambridge History of Mediaeval Political Thought* (Cambridge: Cambridge University Press).

Taubenschlag, R. (1955), *The law of Graeco-Roman Egypt in the Light of the Papyri 332 BC–640 AD* (Warsaw: Panstowowe Wydawnictwo Nantowe).

Temkin, O. (1956), *Soranus, Gynaecology: Translated with an Introduction* (Baltimore: Johns Hopkins).

—— (1991), *Hippocrates in a World of Pagans and Christians* (Baltimore: Johns Hopkins).

Thébert, Y. (1987), 'Private Life and Domestic Architecture in Roman Africa', in P. Veyne (ed.), *A History of Private Life, i. From Pagan Rome to Byzantium* (Cambridge, Mass.: Belknap).

Thomas, K. (1989), review of Boswell 1989, *TLS*, Aug., 25–31.

Thomas, Y. (1980), 'Mariages endogamiques à Rome', *Revue de l'histoire du droit francais et étranger*, 58: 345–82.

—— (1991), 'La Division des sexes en droit romain', in G. Duby and M. Perrot (eds.), *Histoire des femmes, i. L'Antiquité* (Paris: Plon), 103–56.

Treggiari, S. (1981), 'Concubinae', *Papers of the British School at Rome*, 49: 59–81.

—— (1991), *Roman Marriage: iusti coniuges from the time of Cicero to the time of Ulpian* (Oxford: Oxford University Press).

Turpin, W. (1985), 'The Law Codes and Late Roman Law', *Revue internationale des droits de l'antiquité*, 32: 339–53.

—— (1988), '*Adnotatio* and Imperial Rescript', *Revue internationale des droits de l'antiquité*, 35: 285–307.

Van Dam, R. (1985), *Leadership and Community in Late Antique Gaul* (Berkeley, Calif.: University of California Press).

van Eijk, T. H. C. (1972), 'Marriage and Virginity, Death and Immortality', in C. Kannegiesser (ed.), *Epektasis: Mélanges J. Daniélou* (Paris: Beauchesne), 209–35.

Verdery, K. (1988), 'A Comment on Goody's *Development of the Family and Marriage in Europe*', *Journal of Family History*, 13/2: 265–70.

Verdon, M. (1988), 'Virgins and Widows: European Kinship and Early Christianity', *Man*, NS 23: 488–505.

Vikan, G. (1984), 'Art, Medicine and Magic in Early Byzantium', *Dumbarton Oaks Papers*, 38: 65–86.

—— (1990), 'Art and Marriage in Early Byzantium', *Dumbarton Oaks Papers*, 44: 145–63.

Vogel, K. (1967), 'Byzantine Science', in J. M. Hussey (ed.), *The Byzantine Empire, pt. II. Government, Church, and Civilization* (Cambridge Medieval History, iv; Cambridge: Cambridge University Press), 265–305.

Vogt, J. (1974), *Ancient Slavery and the Ideal of Man* (ET; Oxford: Blackwell).

Vogt, K. (1987), 'La Moniale folle du monastère des Tabennésiotes: Une interprétation du chapitre 34 de l'*Histoire Lausiaca* de Pallade', *Symbolae Osloenses*, 62: 95–108.

von Heintze, H. (1971), 'Ein spätantikes Mädchenporträt in Bonn. Zur stilistischen Entwicklung des Frauenbildnisses im 4. und 5. Jahrhundert', *Jahrbuch für Antike und Christentum*, 14: 61–91.

Waithe, M. E. (1987), (ed.), *A History of Women Philosophers, i. Ancient Women Philosophers 600 BC–AD 500* (Dordrecht: Nijhoff).

Wallace-Hadrill, A. (1988), 'The Social Structure of the Roman House in the Late Republic and Early Empire', *Papers of the British School at Rome*, 56: 43–97.

Wallace-Hadrill, D. S. (1968), *The Greek Patristic View of Nature* (Manchester: Manchester University Press).

Ward, B. (1975) (trans.), *The Sayings of the Desert Fathers* (Oxford and London: Mowbray).

—— (1987), *Harlots of the Desert: A Study of Repentance in Early Monastic Sources* (Oxford and London: Mowbray).

Waszink, J. H. (1947), *Tertullian: De anima* (Amsterdam: Meulenhoff).

Wegner, J. R. (1988), *Chattel or Person? The Status of Women in the Mishnah* (Oxford: Oxford University Press).

Wicker, K. O'B. (1987), *Porphyry the Philosopher, To Marcella* (Texts and Translations, 28; Graeco-Roman Religion Series, 10; Atlanta: Society of Biblical Literature, Scholars Press).

Wiedemann, T. (1989), *Adults and Children in the Roman Empire* (London: Routledge).

Wimbush, V. W. (1990), (ed.), *Ascetic Behaviour in Greco-Roman Antiquity: A Sourcebook* (Minneapolis: Fortress Press).

Wolff, H. J. (1945), 'The Background of the Postclassical Legislation on Illegitimacy', *Seminar*, 3: 21–45.

—— (1950), 'Doctrinal trends in Postclassical Roman Marriage Law', *Zeitschrift der Savigny-Stiftung* 67, römische Abteilung 261–319.

Wolfskeel, C. (1987), 'Makrina', in Waithe 1987: 139–68.

Wood, C. T. (1981), 'The Doctors' Dilemma: Sin, Salvation and the Menstrual Cycle in Mediaeval Thought', *Speculum*, 56: 710–27.

Yarbrough, A. (1976), 'Christianisation in the Fourth Century: The Example of Roman Women', *Church History*, 45: 149–64.

Youtie, L. C. (1985), 'The Michigan Medical Codex: P. Mich. Inv. 21', *Zeitschrift für Papyrologie und Epigraphik*, 65: 123–49.

GENERAL INDEX

INDEX OF WOMEN

CPSIA information can be obtained
at www.ICGtesting.com
Printed in the USA
FSHW011634300121
78090FS